Puberty Period & You!

A Guide to Understanding Your Changing Body, Emotions & Life

Rebecca DeWitt

Table of Contents

REFERENCES

213

Introduction

Have you ever been curious about what actually takes place in a girl's body when she begins her period? Maybe you've been thinking about asking your parents, sibling, or other family members, but you stumbled over the word "menstruation" every time you tried to use it.

It's OK! No one likes to broach the subject of their own bodily functions, especially one that can seem as mysterious as menstruation. This book will help clarify some common misconceptions regarding this natural part of a girl's life.

This book is not just about periods, though! It's about all the many things teens experience during puberty. Through this book, you'll be guided every step of the way on your journey through puberty, and will be provided with all the information you want and need to know about this phase of life.

We'll get into the nitty gritty of all the changes you will go through, and you'll be armed with the knowledge you need to navigate this time of big shifts in your life. So, let's dive right into it!

1. Your Changing Body

The process by which a person's body starts to mature and change is referred to as puberty. What exactly does it mean to go through puberty?

The only other moment in your life when your body will grow at a quicker rate than it does when you are going through puberty is when you are an infant. During that time, your physical appearance was changing quickly, and you were acquiring new knowledge. During puberty, you will continue to do both of these things, as well as many more. The only difference is that this time you won't have any diapers or a rattle, and you'll have to clothe yourself!

It is vital to keep in mind that puberty is a natural process that occurs in all people and that it's helpful to be aware of the changes that occur during this time before they take place. You will go through the changes that occur during puberty no matter who you are, where you are from, or what gender you are.

Changing times

When a person reaches a certain age, their brain begins to secrete a specific hormone that kickstarts the physical and mental changes associated with puberty. The hormone in question is referred to as GnRH, which stands for gonadotropin-releasing hormone. When gonadotropin-releasing hormone reaches the pituitary gland, which is a pea-shaped organ located just under the brain, the pituitary gland responds by releasing two more puberty hormones into the bloodstream, these are: a follicle-stimulating hormone (FSH for short), and luteinizing hormone (LH for short). Two additional hormones, testosterone and estrogen, are found in the bodies of both men and women. All these hormones exert their influence on various regions of the body, which vary according to the gender of the individual.

In males, these hormones move through the circulatory system and send a message to the testicles, instructing them to start the process of producing testosterone and sperm. The hormone testosterone is responsible for the majority of the physical changes that occur in a boy's body throughout puberty. In order for males to have children, they need to make sperm cells.

The ovaries, which contain eggs that have been there since birth, are the target of FSH and LH in females. The hormones cause the ovaries to start producing estrogen, which is another hormone in the body's hormone system. Estrogen, together with follicle-stimulating hormone and luteinizing hormone, is responsible for a girl's maturation and helps her body become ready for conception.

During puberty, your body is flooded with new hormones, and as a result, your hormone levels begin to approach those of an adult. This transition from adolescence to adulthood marks the beginning of the process known as andropause.

The onset of puberty typically occurs sometime between the ages of 7 and 13 for females and 9 and 15 for males. However, puberty might begin a little bit earlier or a little bit later for some people. Because every person is unique in some way, the onset and progression of puberty occur according to each person's individual biological clock.

Because of this, you may have some friends who appear to be much younger than they actually are or some who appear slightly older.

It's just a phase...of rapid growth

A quick flurry of action, or something that takes place very quickly, is referred to as a "spurt," and a growth spurt is exactly what it sounds like: your body is developing at an accelerated rate. When you hit adolescence, your body goes through a rapid growth spurt that can make it appear like your sleeves are constantly shrinking and your jeans are always above your ankles in preparation for a flood! This growth spurt might last anywhere from two to three years at a time. Some people have a growth spurt that causes them to add up to four inches to their height in a single year.

Your body will not experience any further height increase after the growth that occurs throughout puberty. After that, you will have reached your adult height. But guess what? Your height won't be the only thing that shifts with time.

Taking shape

As it grows a taller, your body will change in other ways as well. You are going to put on weight, and when that happens, you'll begin to observe general changes in the shape of your body as a whole. Shoulders will widen, and guys will develop more muscle throughout their bodies. Their voices will deepen as time goes by. It's possible that some boys will have a slight increase in breast size during puberty, but for the vast majority of boys, this growth will cease by the time they reach adulthood.

Other changes, including the lengthening and broadening of the penis and the expansion of the testicles, will also be noticeable to males during this time. All of these changes indicate that their bodies are maturing and changing in the way that is typical during puberty.

The bodies of girls typically get more curvy. They put on weight around the hips, and their breasts begin to grow. It's possible that one of your breasts will develop faster than the other, but in the vast majority of cases, they will eventually even out. Because of all of this expanding and developing that is taking place, young girls will experience a normal rise in body fat, as well as periodic discomfort beneath the nipples as their breasts begin to grow larger. This is all to be expected, so don't be alarmed!

Girls naturally go through a phase of puberty in which they experience some weight increase, which can make some girls feel uneasy. It is not recommended that young girls engage in restrictive dieting in an effort to halt this natural weight growth. Talk it over with your parents and physician if you ever find that you are unsure of anything regarding your weight or if you are concerned about it.

Breast growth

During the onset of puberty, girls will see the formation of breast "buds," which are little bumps under the nipple, an early symptom of puberty in most girls. It is not unheard of for the growth of one breast to begin before the other. Additionally, it's not uncommon for the breast buds to feel tender or even painful.

A girl's first period typically occurs between two and two and a half years after the development of her breasts, with some variation. This is just another sign that a girl's body is going through puberty and that the hormones responsible for puberty are doing their job properly. Girls and women have two ovaries, which may store thousands of eggs. During the course of a menstrual cycle, one of the eggs is released from one of the ovaries, where it begins its journey down the fallopian tube, and ultimately lands in the uterus (the uterus is also called the womb).

In the moments leading up to when the ovary dislodges the egg, the uterus is busy thickening its lining with additional blood and tissue. If or when the egg is fertilized by a sperm cell, it will continue to grow inside the uterus and become a baby. As it develops, the baby will make use of the additional blood and tissue in order to grow healthily and safely in the womb.

However, the majority of the time, the egg is only traveling through the process without fertilization. Since the uterus does not require the additional blood and tissue after an egg fails to get fertilized, this material is expelled from the body through the vagina during a monthly period. The average length of a period is between 5 and 7 days, and around 2 weeks after the first day of a period, a new egg is released. This marks the midpoint of the menstrual cycle. But don't worry, we'll get into how periods work in more detail later in this book!

Hair, hair, and even more hair!

To be fair, perhaps it doesn't appear everywhere, but the appearance of new hair in areas where it had previously been absent is one of the earliest indicators that a child is approaching puberty.

Under their arms and in their pubic regions (on and around the genitals) is where hair growth first starts for both boys and girls. The hair growth will be light and sparse at first. After that, as you go through adolescence, it gets thicker, longer, heavier, and naturally darkens. After a certain amount of time, boys' facial hair begins to develop as well.

Acne

Acne, often known as zits, is a common skin condition that occurs throughout adolescence. Puberty hormones are a major contributor to acne breakouts. Acne often appears during the early stages of puberty and may continue into adolescence (the teen years). You can get pimples on your face, upper back, or upper chest. Maintaining a clean skin care routine is beneficial in keeping acne under control, and a visit to the dermatologist can yield some helpful recommendations for reducing acne if you are having difficulty controlling it.

Body odor

When they reach puberty, a lot of young people become aware that the way their body smells starts to change, and the new smell is not a particularly pleasant one! Body odor is responsible for that stench, and everyone has it, so you're not alone. When you enter puberty, the hormones that cause puberty have an effect on the glands in your skin, and those glands produce compounds that have an unpleasant odor. These compounds are responsible for the smell teens often give off.

The question now is, what can you do to stop smelling this way? It's tough to eliminate body odour completely, but keeping yourself and your clothes clean is a smart strategy for reducing any unpleasant odors. A daily shower is recommended, preferably in the morning or the night before school, and so is wearing clean clothes. Using deodorant (or deodorant that also contains antiperspirant) on a daily basis is another great way to help control body odor.

Vaginal discharge

When a person reaches puberty, they will experience a number of different body changes, all of which are perfectly normal. This is true for both boys and girls. Girls may observe and feel a white discharge that looks similar to mucus coming from the vagina. This is merely another indication that your body and hormones are going through a transitional period and does not indicate that anything is amiss.

Erections will start to occur for the boys (when the penis fills with blood and becomes hard). Erections can occur in boys and men for no apparent reason at all, but they most commonly occur when they fantasize and think about sexual topics. It is possible for boys to have what is known as nocturnal emissions (also known as wet dreams), which occur when a boy's penis becomes erect while he is sleeping and he ejaculates. When a boy ejaculates, semen is expelled from the penis; semen is a fluid that contains sperm and is expelled during ejaculation. This is the reason why they are referred to as wet dreams; they take place while you are asleep, and when you wake up, either your underwear or the bed may be slightly damp. As a boy approaches adulthood, the likelihood of having wet dreams decreases, and finally they disappear entirely. Boys may also notice a change in their voice. Their voices may "crack" when speaking, which is another natural part of the aging process and will eventually lead to a deeper tone.

Puberty & your period

See if any of this rings a bell: one morning, you wake up to find that you have grown in height and circumference overnight. It's nighttime and you notice through your nightgown that your breasts have grown larger. When did that happen? What happened to your appearance a few weeks ago? After a few more weeks have gone by, you may also find hair growing in previously hairless areas. You've overheard the other girls in school discussing when they first got their periods, and now you're curious about when it could happen to you. You go from feeling self-assured to feeling vulnerable over the span of a single day. Where did this all come from? Well, the answer is that you've now entered the world of puberty!

In a nutshell, puberty is the process through which your body and mind begin to mature. Although both sexes experience puberty, girls often start going through puberty earlier than their boys do.

So, what exactly is triggering this physical transformation? Well, it's actually pretty simple: hormones! In fact, the primary hormone that is responsible for all of the changes that are occurring in your body as a girl is estrogen. The onset of puberty brings about a number of changes for girls, let's check some of these out below.

Height and weight gain

Around the age of nine, girls start reaching their full adult height growth of about 17–18%. Around this time you are, as the saying goes, "all hands and feet." In a natural order, your trunk develops after your limbs do. Around the time of their first period (also known as "menarche,") girls have often reached their full height, although this can vary.

During puberty, most girls also experience weight increase. There can be an accumulation of fat in the upper body, particularly the arms, thighs, and back. You'll notice a widening of your hips and a narrowing of your waist.

Breast growth

In girls, the appearance of breasts is a precursor to full-fledged puberty. This may occur earlier, in some girls as young as 9, or later in others. A "training bra," which is a soft bra with no real support, is something you could start wearing if you're feeling self-conscious or uncomfortable with this new change.

Discuss getting a training bra with your mother, older sibling, or any other person you feel comfortable talking to about such things. They can make sure you get one that makes you feel good in what you're wearing and fits you properly.

Puberty and girls

Puberty may be a challenging period for young girls. Those who reach puberty at a younger age may experience feelings of embarrassment regarding their newly developed curves. Those who mature at a slower rate than their contemporaries experience a sense of isolation. Gaining weight during adolescence is perfectly normal, but due to societal pressures, it's not uncommon for young girls to wonder, "Am I too fat?" A negative perception of their own bodies can put someone at risk for developing an eating disorder (boys, too).

In order to combat this, it's important to talk to the trusted adults in your life to let them help you develop positive feelings and a healthy relationship with your body and with food.

Accumulation of hair

While for most young girls the appearance of breasts is the first noticeable change marking the start of puberty, another early sign of puberty in girls is an increase in hair growth on the arms, legs, armpits, and genital area.

If you choose to shave, choosing the best razor for shaving sensitive areas like your legs and underarms is something you should discuss with your parents or other trusted adults, so that you can learn how to do this properly without cutting yourself.

It's important to note that not all girls and women remove their hair. In some societies, being unshaven in places like the armpits and the legs is considered to be a positive trait. What is best and most comfortable for you is up to you to determine.

The start of your period (menstruation)

Most girls start menstruating shortly after they reach puberty and develop breasts. Menstruation typically begins between the ages of 11 and 12, although it can begin at any time and at any age during this time in your life. In a typical menstrual cycle, the flow is heavier on days two and three, and lighter from day four onward.

Menstruation is a perfectly normal part of a girl's life, and there's no need to feel ashamed about exploring this natural phenomenon! If you need to talk to someone about your period, don't hesitate to talk to your mom or another trusted adult, or even an older sibling who has already experienced it and can give you some advice or answer your questions.

During your period you will need to use a tampon or sanitary pad. Having your mom (or another trusted adult) buy and demonstrate the use of these items is a great idea to help you feel more comfortable. If you get your period unexpectedly during the school day, it helps to be prepared by carrying pads or tampons in your locker or bag. Don't be embarrassed to approach a female teacher or the school nurse for assistance if you forget or need some help.

Menstrual cramps and bleeding

During your period, your body produces more hormones than usual, which can lead to painful cramping. This cramping is a result of a contraction of the uterine muscular tissue.

You might try placing a heating pad or hot water bottle on your stomach to help with cramping. Acetaminophen (Tylenol), ibuprofen (Advil), and naproxen sodium (Aleve) are all effective pain relievers that can also be used during your period. Always follow the instructions on the label to ensure you don't over-consume these medications. Talk with your parents and paediatrician about alternative treatment choices if you have menstruation cramps that are so severe that they cause you to miss school.

Mood swings

Your period can also come with mood swings and this can be attributed to the hormonal changes that occur during puberty. Irritability is often a symptom experienced during PMS, which refers to "premenstrual syndrome." PMS is a completely normal part of the period process, and PMS symptoms typically subside after your period begins.

If you want to feel better emotionally and physically during PMS and your period, exercising can help. However, it might also be a good idea to talk to your doctor if you've seen a significant drop in your mood with no improvement.

If a girl reaches puberty before her peers, she may feel less confident about herself and her physique. If a girl reaches puberty at a later age than her pals, she may feel isolated. It's important to know that although all girls experience these changes, some may start earlier or later. Everyone is on their own journey, so no need to compare yourself to others! Knowing what's occurring within your body will help you cope with these transitions.

Maintaining a healthy menstrual cycle requires a commitment to a balanced diet, regular exercise, adequate rest, and a low stress level. Regular check ups with your primary care physician will also help you feel your best and give you access to an expert should any issues arise.

Although puberty may present many problems, as long as you're guided through it, you'll be able to navigate them fairly easily!

Even though the timing can be unpredictable, most girls will have their first period between between two and three years after the development of their breast buds. It is essential to note that having periods is a natural and expected part of growing up and it is completely appropriate to ask questions and engage in conversation regarding menstruation. Given that a young person's first period can begin at any time without warning, there is a possibility that this will cause anxiety for some of them. This concern can be alleviated to some degree by familiarizing yourself with the resources available at school, including the school nurse.

When some girls get their first period, they may experience bright red blood, while other girls may simply experience spotting with a reddish-brown discharge; both of these scenarios are normal. Periods may become unpredictable in the first few years as the body adjusts to the rapid physiological changes that occur during this time. Some people will have periods once a month, while for others, periods will occur less frequently. Additionally, the average length of time between periods might range anywhere from 21 to 35 days.

Adapting to change

The changes that hormones bring about on the outside of your body are paralleled by the changes that they bring about on the inside of your body. Your mind is adjusting to all of the new hormones at the same time that your body is doing so. Puberty might bring on feelings of disorientation and intensity of emotion that you have never felt before. There's a chance that you're feeling apprehensive about how your body is changing.

It's possible that you'll feel really sensitive or become agitated very easily. Some teens have an increased tendency to lose their cool and direct their ire toward their families or friends.

Dealing with all of these different feelings can be challenging at times. Most of the time, individuals do not want to make you feel badly or for you to become unhappy. It's possible that your "puberty brain" is merely attempting to adjust, and that your family and friends aren't the ones to blame for your irritability. Even while it may feel challenging at first, the process of adjusting to the change will, over time, become much easier. It might be helpful to talk to someone about how you're feeling and share the load of it with them, whether it's a friend or, even better, a parent, an older sibling, or another adult who's been through it all before.

It's possible that you'll have brand new, baffling emotions towards sexuality, along with an abundance of questions. When your body starts producing adult hormones like estrogen and testosterone, it's a sign that it's preparing you for new responsibilities, like the ability to bear children of your own some day. For this reason, it is essential to make sure that all of your queries are answered so you can make informed, safe and responsible choices.

It is natural to experience feelings of embarrassment or anxiety when discussing sex and sexuality; however, you must ensure that you have all the information you need. Some teens are able to get all of their questions regarding sexuality answered by talking to their parents about it. But if the topic of sex and sexuality make you uncomfortable when discussing it with your parents, there are many other trustworthy professional adults with whom you can discuss it, such as your doctor, a school nurse, a teacher, a school counselor, or another responsible adult with whom you feel at ease having this conversation.

Height changes

The average growth spurt for girls occurs earlier in life than it does for most boys. Typically, a girl's height will increase at its most rapid rate between the time when her breasts first begin to develop and approximately six months before she will start having periods. Once a girl has experienced her first period, the rate at which she will continue to mature has already begun to slow down. After a girl has her period, she will often grow an additional 1-2 inches, but any additional height gain after that is far less common. Her hips will also become wider, but her waist may become narrower as she gets older.

Other common changes

During puberty, acne affects a large percentage of young people. This may be connected to changes in the levels of certain hormones that occur throughout this time. Teens (both boys and girls) often start using deodorants and/or antiperspirants during the beginning of puberty because of the physiological changes that occur during this time, including sweating under the armpits and an increase in body odor. As a result of the increased production of oil and sweat by the skin, teens of this age may find that they need to wash their hair more often and give themselves more frequent showers.

FAQs for parents concerning girls and their changing bodies:

According to what I've heard, the average age at which a girl experiences her first period is becoming lower and lower. Is that the case?

Concerns have been raised regarding this topic. The short response to this inquiry is "maybe." Over the past 150 years, there has been a significant downward trend in the age at which puberty begins, which is likely attributable to advancements in nutrition. Less is known about the tendencies seen in puberty over the past 40 years. According to the findings of a number of research studies, puberty is beginning sooner in both the United States and Europe.

Very small babies often reach puberty at a younger age than expected, and the reasons for this are not well understood. Additionally, obesity is a risk factor for onset of puberty at an earlier age. This is partly due to the fact that body fat plays a role in the way the body processes hormones like estrogen.

In general, additional knowledge and research is required on this subject in order for us to have a complete understanding of these patterns and the potential reasons that they exist.

My kid is concerned that she will put on weight as she enters puberty. How can I help her understand that it's natural for adolescents to put on weight throughout puberty?

As a girl goes through puberty, she will experience an increase in the total percentage of body fat as well as an increase in the amount of fat that will be added to her hips and breasts as a result of the rising estrogen levels in her body. However, weight gain that is excessive in comparison to what is normal during puberty can be cause for concern. Your child's paediatrician will check to see whether her weight increase is above the 85th percentile on her growth chart or if her body mass index (BMI) is higher than that. Both of these may indicate that your child is overweight. However, the pattern of weight increase as a whole is more essential than any one number.

When considering a healthy lifestyle and gaining weight, it is important to keep in mind that habits such as physical activity and good eating are developed at a very young age.

The same is true for the formation of preferences for unhealthy foods and excessive amounts of screen time. Make an appointment with your physician to get some pointers on how to include healthy routines into the daily activities of your family and try to demonstrate a good and healthy mentality, as well as balanced practices when it comes to food and body weight.

Even though she has yet to get it, I want to make sure that my daughter is ready for when she gets her first period. When is the right time to bring up the subject of periods with her?

The appearance of breast buds is an excellent occasion to have a conversation about the bodily changes that are still to come. Insist on the fact that having periods is completely normal, that they are a part of the natural process of puberty unfolding, and that there is absolutely no reason to be embarrassed or ashamed about them. The onset of painful periods might make some young women anxious, as does the possibility that their peers will learn about it. Even though every girl is different, there is a good chance that some of the worry that girls may feel about their periods can be alleviated with the right approach and the right information.

It is in your daughter's best interest to start learning about her body as early as possible in the process of puberty. Otherwise, she runs the risk of being surprised or even scared or confused as the changes in her body begin to take place. It is also a good idea to have period products like sanitary pads ready in advance and to demonstrate to her how to use them before she gets her first period. This can be very helpful and will mean she will be well prepared and can help minimize any embarrassment when the time comes.

Discussing puberty in an open and honest manner is encouraged. Respond to any inquiries she might have regarding the changes occurring in her body. Know that paediatricians are also wonderful resources for any questions about puberty that you or your child may have along the way. You may not be required to know every answer, but having someone who can step in and provide the answers you don't have is important.

When is the appropriate time for my daughter to get a pelvic exam?

If they are otherwise healthy, teenagers do not require a pelvic exam until they reach the age of adulthood (21). Research has demonstrated that adolescents who engage in sexual activity do not require the annual pelvic exams and pap smears that were previously advised for them in the past (Torborg, 2018) (Vinekar et al., 2015). Pap smears are examinations that screen for signs of human papilloma virus (HPV) infection, which can lead to changes in the cervix that are both pre-cancerous and malignant. Over the past few years, we have gained a growing amount of knowledge on HPV, including the fact that adolescent patients have a far greater chance of curing their HPV infection on their own, without the assistance of medical professionals. Only in very exceptional circumstances, such as in young people with HIV or immunological weaknesses, is it suggested to get a Pap smear before the age of 21. Pelvic exams are not performed as part of standard medical care, although they may be required in specific circumstances, such as when a sexually active adolescent who is experiencing abdominal pain seeks medical attention.

When should girls begin learning how to perform breast exams on themselves? Will her paediatrician discuss this matter with her and how she should proceed?

Because of the exceptionally low likelihood that teenage girls may get breast cancer, it is not typically necessary for them to undertake breast self-exams. Additionally, their breasts may change as they mature, and it is not uncommon for discomfort and swelling to occur around the time of menstruation. At this time, it is not advised to undergo routine breast self-exams for young patients, and the recommendations for breast self-exams for adults might vary greatly depending on the source.

How can I watch my daughter's growth without violating her desire for privacy?

Make sure you give your daughter plenty of opportunities to talk about how her body is changing as she enters puberty. Openly discussing puberty can help reduce feelings of embarrassment and stigma, which in turn may make your daughter more eager to talk to you about what she is going through during this time in her life. However, there are some children who just do not want to discuss issues of this nature with their parents, and that is perfectly acceptable.

Make it clear to your daughter that you are available to answer any questions she may have and that she has access to reputable sites from which she can obtain information. These include reading materials and classes that teach students about how to maintain a healthy lifestyle. If there are particular issues that are concerning you related to your child's growth or the way that they are transitioning into puberty, your paediatrician will be pleased to discuss these with you and your daughter.

My child is developing too early or too late, why is this happening and what can I do about it?

As a child grows into a teen, their body undergoes puberty, which can be slow or accelerated.. Female puberty is characterized by the emergence of breasts and the onset of menstruation, whereas male puberty is characterized by the enlargement of the genitalia, the lowering of the voice pitch, and the bulking up of the body.

Girls typically enter puberty at the younger age of 11, while boys typically start around 12. While puberty typically begins between the ages of 11 and 15, it can start as early as 8 years old for girls and as late as 14 years old for guys.

Having puberty begin before the typical age of 8 or later than the average age of 14 is not normally cause for alarm, but it is wise to consult a doctor if you have any concerns. Early or delayed puberty may indicate a medical problem that needs to be addressed in some situations.

Precocious puberty, or early puberty, occurs when:

- Puberty in girls begins before the age of 8 years old
- Puberty begins to manifest in boys before the age of 9

The onset of puberty can vary from person to person, with some girls and boys showing certain signs of development earlier than the average. If a girl begins menstruating before the age of 8, for instance, she may not yet have developed breasts. If this happens to your kid, you should take them to the doctor.

Early puberty: causes and risk factors

The root of premature development is not always identifiable. It could simply be a genetic predisposition. On occasion, it might be brought on by:

- An issue originating in the brain, such as a tumor
- Infection, surgery, or radiation therapy that causes brain damage
- Problem(s) with the uterus, ovaries, or thyroid
- A hormonal condition caused by genetics, like Mccune-albright syndrome

Girls are disproportionately affected by premature onset of puberty, and the underlying cause is typically unclear. Boys are less likely to experience this, and it may be more indicative of a deeper problem.

Delayed puberty

When any of the following conditions apply, we speak of delayed puberty:

- By the time a boy reaches the age of 14, he shows no symptoms of testicular development
- If a girl hasn't begun getting her period by the age of 15, or if she hasn't started developing breasts by the age of 13

The causes of puberty delay

The root of delayed puberty development is not always easy to pin down. Possible hereditary factors should be considered. Boys are more likely than girls to experience a puberty delay. From time to time, it can be brought on by:

- Chronic conditions, like CF (Cystic Fibrosis), DM (Diabetes Mellitus), or CKD (Chronic Kidney Disease).
- Nutritional deficiencies, whether as a result of an eating disorder or a medical condition like Cystic Fibrosis or Celiac disease
- A disorder involving the endocrine system's four major glands (the uterus, the testes, the thyroid, or the pituitary)
- Variations in sexual maturation, such as those caused by androgen insensitivity syndrome

- The result of a genetic condition such as Klinefelter syndrome or Kallmann syndrome

Developing in their own way

Since no two people are exactly alike, their paths to adulthood will not be identical to one another. When going through puberty, no two people are at the exact same stage, and how fast they change varies greatly depending on the person. It's possible that some of your child's friends are developing curves, but they haven't got any just yet. It's possible that their closest friend's voice has matured over the years, but your child is convinced that they still have the high, squeaky voice of a child. Perhaps they may also wish to stop being the tallest girl or the only boy who has to shave.

But in the long run, everybody will get there in their own time, and it's important to let them know that the gaps between them and their pals will disappear. They should bear in mind that there is no "correct" or "incorrect" way to look at puberty. We are all different, both on the inside and the outside, and that is what makes us human!

2. Taking Care of Your Body

Hygiene refers to the practice of keeping your outward appearance clean and well-groomed. Maintaining your health means caring for your physical being.

There are many social, psychological, and emotional benefits to having a clean and healthy personal hygiene routine. It helps keep germs away that could cause illness or infection, and it helps keep body odor in check. Maintaining high standards of personal cleanliness can also boost feelings of well-being, assurance, and satisfaction with your physical appearance.

Puberty is a time when the body generates more hormones, which can lead to an increase in sweat, oil, and body odor, making it especially important to maintain good personal hygiene practices during this time.

Why is good hygiene necessary?

Hygiene is simply how we keep our bodies clean. While we might not be entirely free of germs, if we have a good hygiene routine we are, at the very least, mostly free of the germs that are potentially dangerous and could lead to sickness. Poor hygiene can lead to a wide variety of preventable ailments, including tooth decay, skin infections, and many others.

Our hygiene practices can also affect our social relationships. People generally, and adults in particular, anticipate that others will be clean. Having good hygiene makes it possible for us to have more favorable interactions with other people. Being in close proximity to someone who has offensive breath or body odor can be an incredibly unpleasant experience.

Maintaining good personal hygiene is an indication that you value and care for yourself. In addition to this, maintaining a neat appearance is a respectful gesture toward other people with whom you are interacting.

Personal grooming and hygiene

When it comes to what defines good personal hygiene, various families will have various standards or norms that they adhere to. Some households expect their members to take a shower every day and keep their hair neatly combed, while others may choose to opt for less rigorous rules. No matter what, at this age, because you are going through so many hormonal changes that affect the way your body smells, it's a good idea to take daily showers and wear clean clothes. Doing this will allow you to maintain a good foundation for practicing good hygiene.

If your skin is overly dry, taking a shower once every few days is fine (taking a shower too frequently removes the natural oils that protect the skin), but skipping more than might be excessive, especially if you are active, which will cause you to sweat. Shampooing should be done anywhere from once a week to once every other day, depending on the type of hair you have.

The choice of whether to use deodorant or antiperspirant is a personal one. You can benefit from using an antiperspirant if you have a problem with excessive perspiration. However, overuse of antiperspirants should be avoided at all costs because they have the potential to obstruct the sweat glands located under the arms.

If you take a shower every day and don't think deodorant is required, then go right ahead and skip it! Some households, out of worry for the chemicals contained in deodorant, may choose instead to purchase products that are made from natural materials (or skip the step entirely).

Dental hygiene

Maintaining a healthy oral hygiene routine will assist in the prevention of a range of illnesses. When you brush your teeth, some of the bacteria that are present in the mouth and can lead to bad breath are removed. Cavities and gingivitis (an infection of the gums) are only two of the many diseases and ailments that can be avoided by eliminating this bacteria.

When you floss, you get rid of the bacteria and food particles that are stuck in the spaces between your teeth. If those germs are not removed, they can enter the bloodstream and even cause heart disease. Additionally, they can cause tooth decay and gingivitis, which is an inflammation of the gums.

Because it eliminates these potentially harmful germs, regular flossing has been proven in research to have the potential to extend life expectancy.

Shaving

Many young women, around the time they enter middle school, express an interest in shaving their legs and armpits for the first time. It is a matter of personal preference; there is no physiological need to remove hair from the armpits or legs. If shaving is preferred, here are a few pointers:

Start with a clean, sharp razor. Apply some shaving cream or gel after wetting the skin first. Shaving dry skin can cause it to become irritated and scratchy. When the skin is already wet, shaving could go more smoothly if you do it in the shower or the bathtub. Using shaving gel or cream on the skin works as a buffer and can help prevent cuts from occurring.

Use mild pressure when shaving. If you apply too much pressure to the razor, you can end up accidentally cutting yourself, which you don't want! Take special precautions to prevent nicking the flesh when working around the knees and ankles.

Rinse your razor well after you have finished shaving, and store it in a clean, dry place in between shaves to keep bacteria away from the blade. As the blade begins to become dull with use, either the whole razor or just its blade should be replaced. The skin is more prone to be pulled, scraped, and irritated when the blade is dull.

Razors are not to be shared! The transmission of pathogens like Staphylococcus Aureus, and the development of skin infections can result from sharing a razor.

Electric razors are also an option. There are electric razors available that are tailored to the needs of girls and women. Although they are less likely to produce cuts in the skin, these might nonetheless irritate the surface of the skin, so the same caution and instructions should be used with these.

Finally, remember that it is a matter of personal preference, not an indication of one's level of hygiene, whether or not one chooses to shave.

Grooming

When it comes to personal hygiene, teens have a wide variety of options to choose from. It's possible that you'll need to have a conversation with your parents about the specifics of how to style your hair, how to pluck your eyebrows, how to trim (or paint) your nails, how to wash your face, how to manage acne, and how to apply cosmetics.

As a basic standard, changing your clothing on a regular basis (or whenever they become dirty, sweaty, or soiled) and doing your laundry are good practices to other important maintain good hygiene. In addition, it is a good idea for you to make it a practice to keep your room neat, make your bed, and keep your sheets clean, and generally pick up after yourself on a regular basis.

Menstruation

Once you get your period, it is important that you know the correct way to use hygiene products, including tampons, sanitary pads, and menstrual cups. Learning to keep track of your period can also help you anticipate when your period will arrive, allowing you to avoid being caught off guard and be prepared for bleeding. Talking to your parents or trusted adults early about what's to come is key.

Exercise

When children reach their teenage years, they frequently lose interest in activities that require physical movement. They have a lot of things going on in their lives, like school, homework, friends, and even part-time jobs, so they have to juggle a lot of things and have less "play" time than they did as children.

On the other hand, engaging in regular physical activity might make you feel more energized, focused, and optimistic and help you manage your mental health and deal with the stresses that can come with being a teen.

Physical activity during the teen years

Center for Disease Control (CDC) guidelines for physical exercise for adolescents indicate that teens should get at least one hour each day of moderate to vigorous physical activity. Along with the following:

Aerobic exercise, in which participants engage their larger muscle groups and keep moving for a certain amount of time, should make up the majority of the physical activity. Activities such as jogging, swimming, and dancing are all examples of aerobic activity.

Any action that ranges from moderate to vigorous counts toward the goal of sixty minutes of physical activity. At least three times per week, you should participate in some form of physical activity that helps build your bones and muscles.

Teenagers have many opportunities to be physically active, including participation in sports and organized exercise programs, which often include activities designed to develop muscles and bones. Lifting weights, provided that it is done under the guidance of an experienced adult, can assist in developing strength and reduce the risk of sporting injuries.

Skating, football, meditation, swimming, dancing, or even just kicking a ball in the driveway are all activities that teens can participate in to improve their physical health, provided that they have the chance to, and the interest in doing so. Teenagers can include physical exercise into their day-to-day lives by doing things like walking to school, getting an active part-time job, or doing tasks around the house.

For parents: encouragement of physical activity in teens

Teenagers should be able to make their own decisions on the types of physical activities they choose to participate in, and parents should respect those decisions. Give teenagers a choice of activities to choose from since they want to exercise their independence. Insist that it is not important what they do; all that matters is that they are active. Once they get going, many teens find that the improved sense of well-being, less stress, enhanced strength, and increased vitality that come with exercise are well worth the effort. As a consequence of this, some teens might start engaging in regular physical activity without the encouragement of a parent.

The activities need to be enjoyable if the teenagers are going to maintain their motivation. Provide your teen with tools and transportation, where needed or possible. It is important for adolescents to have opportunities to participate in activities with their peers since their peers can play an important and positive role in their life.

You can make it easier for your teen to maintain an active lifestyle by finding an activity that is adaptable to his or her time constraints. There's a chance that your adolescent won't have enough time to participate in a team sport either at school or in a league in the community. However, many fitness centres cater to teenagers by providing memberships, so students may find time to work out either before or after class.

Some teens will feel more at ease performing exercises that come in the form of active video games or YouTube videos (like tennis or dancing), which are also some viable options. Regardless of the form, it is essential to engage in activities ranging from mild to vigorous on a daily or semi-daily basis.

In addition, all teens should try to limit the amount of time they spend engaging in sedentary activities such as watching television, playing video games, or using electronic devices such as computers, cellphones, or tablets.

Fitness for everyone

Being physically healthy is beneficial for each and every one of us. Maintaining physical fitness can assist in enhancing academic achievement, fostering self-confidence, preventing obesity, and lowering the risk of developing major illnesses later on in life. In addition, engaging in regular physical activity can assist teens in developing the skills necessary to successfully navigate the many mental and physiological obstacles that they encounter on a daily basis.

It's quite fine if you do not have an interest in sports; they aren't for everyone! What's most important is that you get some form of activity in whichever manner you enjoy the most.

In addition to encouraging overall health, exercise can help with stress-prevention and management and help you express and regulate your emotions, which may be more intense at this time in your life. So give it a shot, you might find it hugely helpful and even fun!

Eating habits

When young teens reach the beginning stages of puberty, they frequently report feeling hungry and eating more. This is due to the fact that their bodies go through a significant growth spurt while they are teenagers. A child's growth and development is supported by the additional energy and nutrients that are provided by more food.

It's possible that teens will start experimenting with new eating patterns as well. For instance, it's usual for teens to start eating less fruit and vegetables and more items high in fat and sugar during their teenage years. This could be due to the fact that their peers eat a lot of fast food or convenient foods, that they have their own money to spend on food, or that they are interested in examining their own desires regarding how and what they should eat.

Teenagers acquire the proper nutrition they require for maintaining their health and achieving optimal growth and development when they consume a wide variety of meals from each of the five food groups.

For parents: instilling positive eating behaviors in teens

As teens acquires more autonomy and start to make more of their own decisions regarding eating, parents can support healthy habits by:

- Modelling positive behaviors when it comes to your own relationship with food
- Establishing a dietary environment at home that encourages healthy habits
- Positively discussing the benefits of eating a healthy and balanced diet

Role-modelling

One of the most effective strategies to establish healthy eating habits in teens is for parents to set a good example in terms of the foods they themselves eat and their own eating habits in general. It is crucial to convey that maintaining a healthy lifestyle is a priority for parents as well. This can be accomplished in a variety of ways, such as beginning each day with a healthy breakfast and making it a point to select nutritious and well-balanced meals when going out, as well as when grocery shopping.

One of the most effective ways to enhance a teen's interest in healthy eating and nutrition is to make time for your family to sit down together for nutritious meals on a regular basis and enjoy those meals together. In addition to this, it is a good opportunity for the whole family to gather together and discuss everyone's day, fostering a greater connection despite everyone being so busy.

Making the surrounding food environment more healthy

The following is a list of some tangible steps families can take together to build a healthy eating environment:

- Put teens in charge of helping with the grocery shopping and dinner planning for the household
- Get teens involved in the planning and preparation of at least one healthy dinner for the family each week
- Reduce the number of unhealthy food alternatives available in the home and make it simple for your teen to find nutritious food there

If teens get a head start on learning how to create some easy, nutritious meals now, it will help them make better decisions about what they eat in the future. Additionally, if teens have some control over what is included in the meal, they will be more inclined to consume it.

Talking about it

For parents, the way in which you discuss food has a significant impact on the eating patterns of your child. Instead of concentrating on the consequences of bad eating, you should make an effort to highlight all of the positive aspects of healthy eating. The following suggestions might be of assistance:

Avoid imposing dietary restrictions or labeling foods as "good," "bad," "naughty," or other similar terms. Instead, make striking a balance your goal: maintain a healthy diet the majority of the time, but don't be afraid to indulge in your "occasionally" meals once in a while.

Instil in your child the habit of eating when they are hungry and stopping when they are satisfied. This teaches your child to understand their hunger cues, and distinguish between eating because they are truly hungry and eating because they are bored or sleepy, or emotional, which can lead to overeating. However, you should anticipate that your child will consume a great deal more food as they grow and develop.

Have a conversation with your child about the role that food can play in enhancing concentration, academic performance, athletic ability, and their overall wellbeing. This may have a greater impact on your child than warnings about potential consequences down the road, and it can serve as an incentive for them to make healthier decisions.

Discuss how much you are enjoying and taking interest in the nutritious food you are consuming. Your teen may find that they, too, love eating healthier foods as a result of this.

The dangers of poor dietary habits for teens
Teens' present and future health and wellbeing might be negatively impacted by eating patterns that are unhealthy, such as eating an excessive

amount, not eating enough, or restricting their eating. However, if a teen develops healthy eating habits during these years, they will be able to avoid these hazards to a large extent.

Consuming insufficient food

Teenagers who try to lose weight quickly by going on fad diets or crash diets run the danger of not eating enough food and not getting the nutrients their bodies require for normal growth and development.

Extreme dieting can result in a variety of negative health effects, including exhaustion, impaired concentration, and a loss of bone density and muscle mass. A small percentage of kids experience eating disorders such anorexia, bulimia, and avoidant restrictive eating disorder. Dizziness, excessive exercise, food avoidance, binge eating, and recurrent weighing are some of the indications and symptoms of an eating problem. If you are witnessing these in your teen, it may be time to talk to an expert such as your child's doctor in order to get them some help if needed.

Consumption limits imposed

Unless a teen has a food allergy or food intolerance that has been confirmed by a health expert, there is no need to limit their consumption of certain foods such as dairy products or foods that contain gluten.

It is possible that teens can develop nutritional deficiencies and other health issues as a result of eating a restricted diet that was not adequately planned for and/or overseen by a doctor or registered dietician.

For instance, if a teen follows a dairy-free diet for an extended period of time, it's possible that they aren't consuming enough calcium, vitamin D, energy, and protein needed to maintain peak bone mass and bone health.

Sleep

Adolescence is a pivotal time in development. Changes occur in the areas of the brain and body responsible for emotion, personality, social interactions, and intellectual performance as a young person grows into adulthood.

Teens' performance in all areas of their lives relies heavily on sleep, which plays a crucial supporting role at this stage. Unfortunately, studies show that a large percentage of young people do not get enough sleep.

Teens require 8-10 hours of sleep per night, as recommended by both the National Sleep Foundation and the American Academy of Sleep Medicine. Adequate sleep is essential for teens to preserve their health, mental well-being, and academic achievement.

However, there are several obstacles in the way of teens getting the restful sleep they need on a regular basis. When parents and teens are aware of the obstacles they face, they can work together to devise a strategy to ensure teens receive the sleep they require.

Why is sleep important for teens in puberty?

No matter what your age is, getting enough sleep is essential. Teens, however, are still growing, and need quality sleep for optimal mental, physical, social, and emotional growth.

Cognitive abilities and scholastic performance

A good night's sleep can improve your focus, memory, and ability to reason. It sharpens the mind, allowing one to zero in on the most vital details in order to retain knowledge. Sleeping allows for more abstract thought, which can cause a creative spark. Teens absolutely need adequate sleep in order to succeed both academically and creatively.

Teens who don't get enough sleep are more likely to be excessively sleepy and have trouble paying attention in class, both of which can negatively affect their grades and general academic performance.

Sleep and mental health

A lack of sleep can have a negative impact on one's mood, leading to heightened irritation and emotional reactivity. Teenagers, who are adjusting to increased freedom, higher responsibilities, and novel social relationships, are particularly vulnerable to the long-term effects of such decisions.

Negative effects on emotional development due to chronic sleep loss have been linked to an increase in the likelihood of developing both minor and major personality conflicts, as well as more severe mental health issues.

Sleep deprivation in adolescents can raise their risk of suicide, and has been connected repeatedly to mental health problems like anxiety, sadness, and bipolar disorder. Teens who get better sleep may be less likely to develop mental health problems or experience less symptoms of those diseases.

Physical growth and development

A good night's sleep aids the efficient operation of nearly every physiological system. It helps with hormone regulation, speeds up the healing process for injured muscles and tissues, and boosts the immune system.

Adolescence is a time of significant physical development, and sleep deprivation can have severe effects on this process. For instance, research has shown that teenagers who do not get the recommended amount of sleep have an unfavorable metabolic profile, which may put them at an increased risk of developing diabetes down the road, as well as long-term cardiovascular problems.

Making choices and taking chances

The frontal lobe of the brain, which plays a crucial role in self-control, can be negatively impacted by a lack of sleep. Sleep-deprived teens are more prone to drive under the influence, send texts while driving, ride a bike without a helmet, and not use a seatbelt, as has been shown in a number of studies. Teens with sleep deprivation have also been found to be more prone to engage in dangerous behaviors such as drug and alcohol usage, smoking, sexual risk-taking and physical conflict.

Teens who struggle with behavioral issues often struggle in other areas of their lives as well, such as at school and in their relationships with others, including their loved ones.

Injuries and mishaps

Teens who don't get enough sleep are also more likely to suffer serious or fatal accidents. Drowsy driving is a serious problem, because it increases the likelihood of accidents. Science has shown that not getting enough shut-eye can slow response times in a way that's comparable to drinking heavily. Teenagers' inexperience behind the wheel and their propensity for distraction both increase the dangers of driving when sleepy.

Why do many teens suffer from sleeplessness?

Teens need 8-10 hours of sleep per night on average. It takes a toll if you need eight hours of sleep and you get up at 6 a.m. for school, but only go to sleep past 10 p.m. However, many teenagers have problems sleeping at such an early hour since their bodies and brains are wired for a later schedule.

The body's internal sleep schedule shifts during adolescence, causing teens to go to bed later and rise later. The production of melatonin, the body's natural sleep hormone, shifts later in the evening in adolescents as compared to younger children and adults. That's why it's so hard for teenagers to get to sleep. In extreme cases, this lag in the sleep-wake cycle might impair a person's ability to function normally throughout the day. This is referred to as "night owl" or "delayed sleep phase" syndrome.

Teens often have trouble sleeping for other reasons, too. The inability to fall asleep is compounded by the disruption of melatonin production caused by exposure to both bright lights and the blue light emitted by electronic devices. Insomnia is very common, meaning that many people struggle to get to sleep or stay asleep. The inability to fall or stay asleep can be caused by a wide variety of factors:

- Feeling uncomfortable or unwell
- Difficulty falling or staying asleep due to temperature, light, sound, or other environmental disturbances
- Anxiety or tension caused by things like school, friendship, or family issues

- Mental health disturbances including anxiety and depression
- Physical health issues
- Constant inability to rest properly

Occasionally, everyone has problems nodding off. However, if you've been having trouble sleeping for a few weeks or months, you should see a doctor.

Tips for helping teenagers find better sleep

If a teen is experiencing trouble sleeping, they should first discuss their sleep habits with their family doctor. Their paediatrician can help find the root of the problem and prescribe the best treatment for them.

Medication may be considered for teens with sleep disorders, although this usually isn't necessary to help them obtain a better night's rest.

Teens would do well to evaluate and enhance their sleep hygiene (the conditions and the manner in which they sleep). Here are some suggestions for strategies and practices to encourage sound sleep that may be helpful:

- Including a set eight-hour sleep time in your daily routine and sticking to it, weekdays and weekends alike
- Establishing a regular routine in the hour or so before bedtime has been shown to improve both sleep quality and the time it takes to fall asleep
- Not drinking any caffeinated or energy beverages after 2 p.m.
- Putting away electronic gadgets at least half an hour before bedtime and placing them on mute to minimize the temptation to check them in the middle of the night
- Sleeping on a bed with a good mattress and comfortable pillow

Maintaining a calm, dark, and peaceful sleeping environment

Modifications to sleep hygiene are sometimes incorporated into cognitive behavioral treatment for insomnia (CBT-I), a talk therapy for sleeping issues that has shown promise in adults and may be useful for teenagers. CBT-I helps people get better sleep by retraining their brains to think in more positive ways about sleep and by teaching them to adopt new, more effective habits.

For parents: how can you facilitate improved sleep patterns for your teens?

Since many parents don't recognize that their teenagers are having sleeping problems, asking them about it is often the first step.

Teens can benefit from parental encouragement to see a doctor, and from assistance in implementing healthy sleep habits. Although they may put up a fight, teens whose parents enforce a strict nighttime routine tend to get more sleep and show less signs of sleepiness during the day.

If parents want schools to start later, they can try lobbying their school districts. Some school districts have tried out delayed starts and seen improvements in attendance and test scores as a result.

Parents can also help by ensuring teens aren't over-scheduled and taking on responsibilities that might cause stress and prevent them from getting enough sleep.

3.   Emotions

It's natural for a person's emotions to shift as they go through puberty. Puberty has repercussions on more than just your physical body. In this chapter we'll explore some of the most common emotional changes experienced during this time in your life.

Emotional changes throughout adolescence and puberty

During adolescence, every teen goes through a variety of emotional ups and downs. When you reach puberty, things have the potential to become quite emotional, and this can happen in both positive and problematic ways.

Feeling excessively sensitive

It is normal for a person to experience feelings of uneasiness and become overly sensitive about their physical appearance during puberty. This is because your body goes through numerous changes during this time, and it is natural for you to feel uncomfortable about these changes! Because of this, you can become easily annoyed, lose your temper, become irritable or have feelings of depression. These feelings are all perfectly normal and nothing to be ashamed of, but it will be helpful for you to be conscious of the changes in your conduct and discuss them with a person who you feel comfortable talking to about the topic.

Searching for one's own identity

You are now in the process of maturing into a young adult, therefore it is natural that you would be curious about the qualities and characteristics that set you apart from other people. In addition to this, there is a common pattern in which you are more likely to spend time with your friends than with members of your own family during these years.

From a psychological point of view, it's possible that it's because your pals are going through the same confusing time you are and you feel understood by them. You might start trying to figure out what makes you unique in comparison to other people and where you stand in the grand scheme of things. In the long run, this will make it easier for you to establish your own identity apart from your parents and family in a healthy way, but right now it might feel like it's just creating more distance between you and them.

Discomfort is common

Puberty is a transitional period in which you are neither fully an adult nor a young child anymore; as a result, it might bring about feelings of uncertainty or discomfort. During a moment of transition, you may find that you start to question your parents and the way they do things. You are learning about yourself and the world around you, and this kind of questioning is normal, but it may lead to conflict and disagreements with your parents, making life a little more unpredictable for all of you.

This unpredictability is brought into sharper focus whenever there is also a change in the expectations that those closest to you have of you. It is possible that you will be asked to take on bigger responsibilities than were placed on you when you were a child. This process will follow its own course and be determined in large part by how you react to the challenges that you are now facing. Eventually, you will mature into your various new roles and become more certain about who you are.

Having a new perspective on your peers

When you reach your teenage years, one of the most significant aspects of the mental shifts that take place is that you begin to view your relationships in a different light. This may involve developing deeper, more emotional relationships with your existing circle of pals. Not only are friends people you can have fun with, but you now may find that you can also confide in them in greater, deeper ways, unlike when you were younger, when friends were more about someone to play with. Put your friendships to the test by demonstrating that you can be relied upon and trusted, too. This can also help you develop confidence and a stronger sense of who you are as a person.

It's also possible that you might begin to develop romantic feelings for a person you once only viewed as a friend, which can cause more emotional confusion in general!

Peer pressure

Puberty may also bring with it the issue of peer pressure, and feelings of being influenced by those around you who you want to relate to and be like. Depending on what you see, you might find yourself caring about and picking up on what's in and what's out in terms of what you wear, what you say, and even how you behave.

This can make you feel uncomfortable at times, and it might even cause you to change the things you actually like and don't like, since you are probably still trying to figure these out yourself.

As you develop your own sense of self, you will learn what your own tastes, values and opinions are, and will find that you become less influenced by what those around you are doing and saying.

Not a child, not yet an adult

When you are a teenager going through puberty, you may feel as though you're caught between who you were when you were a child and who you want to be when you grow up. This is because you are somewhere in between! For example, you might have the goal of becoming more independent, but at the same time, you might also be interested in still receiving help from your parents.

One other example of this may be the question of whether or not you want to give up the hobbies and interests you had when you were a child so that you can be more popular with your peers. This might leave you feeling conflicted or unsure what to do, so you might look for clarity from your parents. Or, you want more independence so you want to get a driver's license, but still need help and guidance from your parents on how to go about getting this. It's normal to be stuck between your younger self and your maturing self, but it can cause you to feel more confused!

Mood swings

In addition to the uncertainty and competing thoughts you're experiencing, you may also find that your mood changes frequently and abruptly. This may be one of the most difficult aspects of puberty. For instance, your mood can quickly go from one extreme to the other, going from feeling confident and joyful to feeling frustrated and unhappy in a very short period of time. A person's mood is said to be "prone to swings" when they experience such changes frequently. The fluctuating levels of hormones and other bodily changes that occur during puberty may be to blame for the occurrence of mods swings in many teens.

A newfound self-awareness

The beginning of puberty can occur at different times for different people. As a result, the manner in which you mature may differ from the way your peers mature. This may cause you to become more hyper aware about how you're coming of age and your changing body in relation to your peers.

Due to the fact that girls develop more quickly and at a younger age than boys, the effects of these physical changes are amplified for them. The changes that take place in their bodies, such as the development of breasts and the broadening of the hips are more visible, which can make them more self-conscious about their appearance in front of their peers who are the same age as them.

Experiencing sexual urges or desires

After you have completed the puberty stage, you will have reached your sexual maturity (physically-speaking). At this point in your life, you are considered sexually mature (again, in a physical sense) and are able to produce children. One characteristic of sexual maturity is a curiosity, not only about sexuality but also about the bodies of persons to whom one is attracted. When a person reaches puberty, it is natural for both the boy and the girl to experience sexual attraction to people who they feel they want to have a deeper relationship with than "simply friends."

Normal, everyday activities, such as reading about or seeing a romantic scene on television, can also make you feel sexually aroused and excited. These emotions are completely normal, and there is no reason for you to feel guilty or embarrassed about having them.

You may begin to have numerous questions about sex and it's best to talk to a responsible adult whom you trust, such as one of your parents, your doctor, or a counselor about them. You need to find out the answers to your questions and gain the knowledge necessary to make informed and safe decisions when it comes to your body and wellbeing. Having this knowledge does not necessarily mean you should feel pressured to engage in any sexual activity whatsoever, but it will help you be informed and will mean you are able to do so safely whenever you are ready, even if that is not for many years to come.

A change in thinking

As you become older, your comprehension and understanding of situations begins to shift. To put it simply, you've reached the point when you think more like an adult. Your brain is actually expanding, therefore you should put that newfound capacity to good use! You'll find that your perspectives on people and the world in general changes and becomes more complex, and you'll have the opportunity to explore new areas of interest and thought.

A greater ability for self-expression

You'll realize that you're able to express whether you're pleased or sad to other people much more effectively, and sometimes simply speaking things out loud may help give you a better understanding of who you are and what you think. On the other hand, the challenging aspect of this situation is that you are likely feeling more self-conscious, which may cause you to have second thoughts about opening up. Just keep in mind that going through all of this is a normal part of growing up, and that by the time you're done, you'll have a deeper understanding of both your body and your mind.

Your changing brain

You may have heard people say that teens have "raging hormones." However, recent studies inform us that although hormone levels do increase beginning in the early stages of puberty, they do not play a significant role in the more intense emotions that teenagers may occasionally feel. Instead, the majority of the changes that occur during this time period are connected with the maturing process of the brain.

The circuits in the brain of a teen are undergoing reorganization and maturation, particularly those circuits involved in the processing of emotions, in social relationships, and in both taking risks and being rewarded for those risks.

Different regions develop and reach their full potential at various times

The limbic system, which is the part of the brain that is responsible for processing feelings, goes through some changes during this stage of life. This can give the impression that teenagers are more emotionally unstable and reactive. For instance, they may experience a greater number of "peaks and valleys."

As teens age and reach their twenties, the prefrontal cortex is still evolving, which is important since it plays a role in reasoning, rational thinking, decision-making, and the regulation of emotions and impulses. Teenagers' capacities to think clearly and make sound choices are fine-tuned as their neural networks connecting the prefrontal brain and the limbic system grow more efficient. This development also contributes to the improvement of teenagers' abilities to control intense emotions and impulses. Over time they improve their ability to manage these in a way that is both controlled and reliable.

Teen emotions

When teenagers reach puberty, they may have a more heightened and intense experience of feelings and often become more emotionally sensitive.

Their highs may appear to be higher, while their lows appear to be lower. The way that they respond one day could be very different from the way that they respond the next day. This is due to the fact that they are still developing the skills necessary to manage powerful feelings and communicate these in ways that are appropriate for their age. As they mature, teens become more likely to take a step back and think about how they want to react to a situation before they do so. This is because the parts of their brain that govern their emotions are maturing, and they have more experience managing strong feelings.

Teenagers often have a strong sense of self-awareness and a heightened sensitivity to the feelings and perspectives of others. They come to place a high value on the sense that they are a part of the group and that they are accepted by their peers. They can mistakenly believe that everyone is watching them, because of the way that they are behaving. As meaningful friendships and love connections come and go in their lives, they may experience extreme highs of delight or the lowest lows of misery. Around the time that a person is in their mid-teens, the strong sway of emotions typically begins to lessen, which can be a relief!

Even while more intense feelings are normal at some stages of adolescence, it is imperative that a young person seeks assistance if their emotional responses appear exaggerated, continue for an extended period of time, or if members of their family are concerned about them. For some teenagers, intense emotional responses may be an early indicator of mental health difficulties.

If this is the case, parents should consult a primary care physician before taking any other action on this matter. If treatment is necessary due to mental health concerns presenting at this stage, they can work with the family to provide an appropriate treatment plan.

Helping teenagers develop healthy methods to manage stress and to process ideas and feelings that may overwhelm them is one way that adults, including parents and other trusted adults, may offer support to young people.

For instance, they may encourage teens to engage in physical activity, to practice meditation, or to make music or other forms of art. It is important to note that how adults react to teen outbursts also makes a difference. Even though an adult might have the urge to yell at a frustrated or overburdened teen, doing so is not likely to help settle the situation or resolve the disagreement, nor will it show by example what an appropriate reaction should be. Adults can help teens navigate how to express emotions in a healthy way by demonstrating this via their own actions.

Understanding different points of view

Teenagers have a great capacity for empathizing with the experiences, emotions, and perspectives of others, as well as an awareness of the ways in which these may contrast with their own. As teens begin to have more complex connections, it can be helpful for them to learn how to put themselves in someone else's shoes - in other words, understand the feelings and perspectives of others. To gain a wider and more varied worldview, it will also be beneficial for them to cultivate more tolerance for individuals who have beliefs and interests that differ from their own. This ability and desire to empathize with others will help teens cultivate more compassion, which is a trait that will serve them well throughout their whole lives.

Interpreting the feelings and social cues of others

Babies are able to interpret the feelings demonstrated by the facial expressions of other people shortly after birth. As they mature, they become more skilled in this. The ability to read and process more complex emotions, and to recognize subtle non-verbal signs is something that individuals develop during the adolescent stage of development.

At this stage, teens tend to begin to spend more time with their peers as they become less emotionally reliant on their parents. It therefore becomes more common for them to be aware of what other people think of them and whether or not their contemporaries are sending signals of approval and acceptance or signals to the contrary. If they have the impression that they do not "fit in," they may start to change their behavior and responses in an effort to win the approval of their peers.

This is also a time when teens often begin to develop romantic interests in other people their age. They may be able to detect romantic desire directed toward them, such as a flirty gaze, or evaluate a possible partner's "suitability" as a result of their growing ability to read facial expressions or emotion cues.

Taking care of mental health

The teen years are a special and formative period. Teenagers are especially susceptible to mental health issues, because of the rapid physical, emotional, and social changes that occur during this time. For the health and well-being of adolescents and young adults, it is essential that they be shielded from harm, that they have opportunities to develop their social and emotional skills and their psychological health, and that they have ready access to professional mental health services when and if they need it.

1 in 7 people between the ages of 10 and 19 worldwide suffer from a mental health condition, but these issues are often misdiagnosed or untreated.

Exclusion from social groups, discrimination, stigma (which might make them less likely to seek treatment), educational challenges, risky behaviors, poor health, and violations of human rights are all things that teens with mental health disorders face on a regular basis.

Factors influencing mental health

The adolescent years are pivotal for establishing healthy psychological patterns. Changes in lifestyle, such as getting enough sleep and exercising regularly, as well as learning to cope with difficult situations and to communicate effectively with others and control negative emotions, can have a profound impact. For the sake of their mental health, it's crucial for teens to have a safe and nurturing atmosphere at home, in school, and in the community.

The state of one's mind can be affected by a number of different things. Teenagers' mental health may be negatively affected to a higher extent in proportion to the number of risk factors to which they are exposed. Adversity, peer pressure to conform, and the search for an individual identity are all factors that can add stress during adolescence.

The gap between a teen's present experience and their expectations and hopes for the future can be widened by the effects of media and social conventions. The influence of their family and friends is also very significant. Physical and sexual abuse, bullying, and other forms of victimization, as well as poor living conditions and joblessness, are also all known to have negative effects on mental health.

Poor living conditions, social stigma, discrimination or exclusion, and a lack of access to quality supports and services can all put some teenagers facing these challenges at a higher risk of mental health issues.

Mental and emotional illness

Teenagers have a high prevalence of emotional disorders. Younger teens are more likely to experience depression than their older counterparts, but older teens are more likely to suffer from anxiety disorders (which may involve panic or excessive worrying). Anxiety disorders affect an estimated 3.6% of children ages 10-14 and 4.6% of those aged 15-19. 1.1% of 10-14 year olds and 2.8% of 15-19 year olds are believed to suffer from depression. Rapid and sudden shifts in mood are one characteristic shared by depression and anxiety.

Negatively affecting both school attendance and performance, anxiety and depression disorders can have serious consequences for a student's mental health. Teens experiencing either of these may find themselves withdrawing from society, which often results in even more solitude and isolation.

Advocacy and safety measures

Interventions for promoting mental health and preventing mental health problems include trying to improve teens' emotional regulation skills, providing more positive alternatives to harmful habits, increasing their ability to deal with adversity, and developing their social networks and communities.

Reaching teenagers, especially those most at risk, requires a multi-pronged approach that incorporates a variety of delivery platforms (such as digital media, health or social care settings, schools and/or the community) and techniques.

What you can do

You're in your teens, and you've undoubtedly realized that a lot is happening to you. Your body and emotions are constantly changing, which can cause feelings of instability. As you age and eventually enter the workforce or enter higher education, you may find that you are held to higher standards. It's important that you develop the skills necessary to adapt to the shifting dynamics of your circumstances, as well as your interactions with everyone you come into contact with, including family, friends, co-workers and classmates.

With so much going on, it might be difficult to focus on your mental health, but focusing on taking care of your mental health now will help you in the short and long run.

What exactly does "mental health" entail?
Mental health refers to the notion that if your emotions, and thoughts are healthy, then that contributes to your overall health. Your mind is an

extension of your body, therefore physical health and mental health go hand in hand. Just as you would do what's best for you physically, making smart decisions regarding your lifestyle and surroundings can do wonders for your mental health. Taking care of one's mental health also includes learning how and when to ask for help if you are in need of it.

Consider the impact of what you eat and drink

How you feel physically and mentally may be affected by what you consume. Eating well on a regular basis not only provides you with the fuel you need to get through the day, but it can also help keep your mood steady. If you want to feel better after meals, try these strategies:

Don't skip breakfast

With a full stomach and a positive attitude before leaving the house, your day is already off to a great start after a hearty breakfast!

Stay hydrated

A headache, fatigue, and irritability are all symptoms of dehydration. If you want to stay hydrated throughout the day, especially on hot days or after strenuous activity, you should bring a water bottle with you and sip from it frequently. Make sure you are drinking enough water throughout the day to maintain a good level of hydration.

The effects of sweets

Eating sugary candies, pastries, and beverages can cause a rapid increase in blood sugar, which can make you feel fantastic initially, but will then cause a rapid decrease in blood sugar, which can make you feel sluggish, irritable, and hungry. While these are fine to eat periodically if you enjoy them, try fuelling your body with foods that will not cause these symptoms.

Get moving

Though you may have associated exercise solely with physical health, your brain also benefits from regular physical activity! Feel-good endorphins and other chemicals are released during exercise. Muscle relaxation, breath regulation, and mental distraction are all great potential benefits of exercise.

Every day, if possible, make time to engage in some form of physical activity, even if it's just for ten minutes. It doesn't need to be strenuous and it's not necessary to stick to a strict training regimen in order to reap the benefits of exercise; instead, you should practice whatever physical activity you find most enjoyable. You could go for a jog or a stroll with the dog, dance it out in your room, or do some gentle stretches or whatever form of movement suits your ability and desires.

Learn to handle pressure

The human body reacts naturally and predictably to stressful conditions. There are many sources of stress in life, including forthcoming exams, work or sport commitments, managing friendships and relationships, and just living in general.

The ability to focus and work diligently for short periods of time is a benefit of stress. However, stress becomes harmful when it persists over time and disrupts your ability to unwind. Constant stress can deplete your energy, cause physical symptoms like a headache or stomachache, and even affect your mental health by making you frequently anxious or unhappy. Here are some things you can do to keep your stress levels down:

Take breaks

Plan time into your daily routine to unwind and be completely yourself. During your "me" time, do whatever makes you happy, be it listening to music, watching a TV show, preparing a meal, going for a walk, or singing. Taking a short break, even if you have an upcoming exam or deadline, can improve your productivity and stress when you get back to work and whatever tasks and responsibilities await you.

Practice mindfulness and awareness

Relaxation isn't always something that comes easily, so it's not a bad idea to learn how to do it when you're feeling overwhelmed. The good news is that you can learn ways to help you calm down in stressful situations, and doing so can make your everyday life better as well.

The practice of mindfulness means being fully present in the moment rather than dwelling on the past or anticipating the future. Mindfulness means giving one's whole attention to the activity at hand, no matter how big or small.

Calming the body and mind is what relaxation is all about. Relaxation is a skill that can be practiced daily to help reduce stress and can be drawn upon when needed. Mindfulness practitioners often report increased feelings of calm and a deeper sense of relaxation as a side effect of their efforts to become more aware.

Realize you are not alone

Mental health challenges are quite widespread, and this includes things like eating disorders, depression, and anxiety. Many teens deal with pressures and stress that can cause them to struggle with their mental health.

If you've been feeling overwhelmed by stress, anxiety, sadness, anger, numbness, or a general sense that things "just aren't right" for a while (two weeks or more), know that you don't have to suffer in silence and that there are resources available to help you.

The best thing you can do is talk to a trusted adult about how you're feeling. This might be anyone from a doctor or school counselor, to a trusted teacher or sports coach, or your parents. If you'd rather talk to a stranger first, you can always call a helpline. An online search should help you find a number for one where you live.

Tools for mental health and self-care

Keep in mind that there are many options available to help you feel better, including making adjustments to your lifestyle, attending therapy, and even taking medication if required for managing mental health concerns. Let's have a look at some other tools to help you manage your mental health and care for yourself.

Make some room in your schedule

That's the starting point for almost any self-care strategy. While we all have a need to keep schedules to balance our responsibilities, with everything going on, it can be challenging to carve out time for yourself, but doing so is essential for your wellbeing! It's never too early to establish a new good habit. The majority of the following suggestions won't take up more than fifteen to twenty minutes of your time. Consistency is the most important factor.

Meditation

The old days when people thought meditation was hocus pocus are long gone. Mindful meditation has been shown to positively alter brain structure and function, making it an excellent tool for relieving stress, sadness, and anxiety. You can take a class, read about it, or watch a video to learn how to do it. The best part about meditation is how accessible it is. You don't need any fancy equipment or resources, all you need it a little bit of time and stillness. Whenever you find yourself in need of it, you can do this wherever you happen to be.

Yoga

For thousands of years, people have turned to Eastern forms of exercise like yoga to help them relax, gain flexibility, and feel a greater sense of overall wellbeing. Learning Yoga is best done in a studio, but you may also do it by watching videos online and following along with the instructors. Ease into it and follow the instructions closely to ensure you don't injure yourself or overdo it as a beginner.

Exercise

While Yoga is a form of exercise itself, there is a wide variety of other ways to exercise. Strength training, endurance training, and aerobic exercise are all great options to get your heart rate up and a good sweat going. But merely walking 2 miles a day is a wonderful workout — plus it gets you outside and in nature! In addition to improving your physical health, exercise is a tried-and-true method for alleviating mental health issues like despair and anxiety. Find a form of exercise that you enjoy and that works for your ability and mobility level.

Sleep

Sleep deprivation negatively affects a person's mental, physical, and emotional wellbeing, but getting enough sleep is easier said than done. Teens and young adults often need nine or more uninterrupted hours of sleep every night to feel rested and perform at their best. It's challenging to find time for this among all of your other obligations, but the benefits are well worth the effort. In most cases, if you make an effort to stick to a consistent sleep schedule, your "biological clock" will remember when it's time for you to go to sleep and wake up. Start out by trying to go to bed at the same time every night. Your body and mind will thank you when you start to feel more rested!

Creativity

You probably have a lot of complicated feelings you want to express these days. Well, try picking an artistic or creative pursuit as a means of expressing your emotions. Writing in a diary, penning a poem, sketching, painting, photography, dance, or making music are all examples of ways to get creative and channel and release your emotions. No need for any of it to be perfect, just enjoy the experience of creating something!

Pets

Having a pet can be a great way to practice self-care if you're lucky enough to be able to do so. You'll understand if you have one! We don't often get the chance to spend so much time cuddling with, caring for, and basking in the unconditional affection of a pet, so if you are able to, enjoy the moment.

Socialize

According to research, socializing with friends and discussing your problems, especially any unresolved emotional issues from the past, helps you stay happy and reduces burnout.

Forming bonds with others is crucial for promoting resilience and stimulating the production of hormones and neurotransmitters that contribute to a sense of well-being. As an added bonus, the activities you do with your friends can come in any form. Activities such as making art, experimenting with slime, or playing video games are effective ways to bring people together.

Even though it may seem important to have a large number of friends or "followers" online, the truth is that a small group of truly good friends can make a great impact in your life, because you are able to build deeper and more meaningful bonds and connections.

Enjoy nature

We hold our parks, rivers, and beaches in high regard for good reason. Recall the beautiful sunrises and sunsets you've witnessed, the hikes you've taken, the parks you've biked through, the snow you've played in, and the walks you've taken around your neighborhood. Try to recall the sensation. If we can only take a few minutes out of our day to relax and enjoy the outdoors without worrying about deadlines or being interrupted by our phones, we find that it has a positive effect on our mood.

Put away the devices

This is a tough one! However, the more you practice it the more you will see that it's not necessary to have your phone attached to your side permanently. You might feel like withdrawing or be worried that you'll miss something crucial by not being present, but take a step back and reflect. How many messages, posts or other forms of digital communication can you live without? Plenty, you'll see! If you're constantly bombarded by alerts, taking a vacation from them may be rather welcome.

Be kind

The human brain is hardwired to be kind. The brain's reward chemicals are significantly higher during the act of giving than receiving. Volunteering in community centres, soup kitchens, elderly life centres, children's hospitals, or after-school programs, even in a modest way, can give you the sense (and reality) that you are making a positive impact on the life of someone else.

It's important to develop and implement strategies like those mentioned above to ensure we are able to handle the stresses and challenges life throws at us, while also taking good care of ourselves.

4. Your Period & You

Your period can seem like a mysterious and complicated process. Let's take a look at what exactly takes place during your menstrual cycle and how that affects your mind and body.

What is a period?

Every month, women experience menstruation, which is the natural process of the uterine lining being shed. The act of menstruation is often referred to as a period. During this time, menstrual blood, which is composed of both blood and uterine tissue, is expelled from the body via the vagina after passing through the cervix. When you are bleeding during this time, this is commonly known as "having your period" or being "on your period."

How does a regular menstrual cycle work?

Each month, your body goes through a series of events known as a menstrual cycle in order to become ready for a potential pregnancy. Day one of your period marks the beginning of a new menstrual cycle. Even though 28 days is the typical length, cycles can be anything from 21 to 35 days. However, this does not mean you have your period for 21 to 35 days! Your period itself typically lasts between 5 to 7 days of this entire 21 to 35 day cycle.

Your menstrual cycle is regulated by hormone levels, which fluctuate throughout the course of the cycle. The reproductive system responds to fluctuations in hormone levels, which are produced and released by the pituitary gland in the brain and the ovaries in the reproductive tract at specific times of the menstrual cycle. Let's take a deeper dive into everything that happens during your menstrual cycle:

The period

If you did not become pregnant during your previous cycle, the uterine lining will be shed on day 1 of your new cycle. This shedding is when you bleed, also known as your period. Though the average duration of bleeding is five days, a period that lasts anywhere from 2 to 7 days is still considered normal.

Phase of follicle development

Usually between days 6 and 14, what's known as the "follicular phase" of your cycle occurs. The increase in estrogen causes the endometrium (the uterine lining) to expand and thicken throughout this time. Follicle-stimulating hormone, another hormone, grows follicles in your ovaries. A mature egg will develop in one of the follicles between days 10 and 14.

Ovulation

In a typical 28-day menstrual cycle, ovulation would occur around day 14th. Your ovary will release an egg when another hormone, luteinizing hormone, spikes suddenly. Ovulation is the term for this process.

Luteal phase

You'll be in this stage for around the next 28 days. When an egg is fertilized, it leaves the ovary and makes its way down the fallopian tubes toward the uterus. Pregnancy preparation begins in earnest when progesterone levels rise and help line the uterus. Pregnancy results from a fertilized egg attaching itself to the uterine wall after being fertilized by a sperm. If conception does not take place, the uterine lining will become thinner and you will experience a monthly period.

When does your period (menstruation) usually start?

The average age a person begins menstruation is 12. A girl might start menstruating at age 8, but it can start as late as age 16. Menopause, which typically happens between the ages of 51 and 55, is when women stop having periods. During menopause, egg production ceases (you stop ovulating). After a woman has gone through menopause, which is defined as a year without having a period, she is no longer able to get pregnant.

What are the signs of a healthy menstrual cycle?

- Moodiness
- Difficulty falling asleep
- An urge to eat
- Leg and back cramps
- Bloating
- Experiencing tenderness in the breasts
- Acne

What signs should I look out for?

If any of the following apply to you, it could be time to see a doctor:

- You are 16 years old and you still haven't begun menstruation
- You have a quick end to your period
- You have had longer bleeding episodes than usual
- Your period is much heavier than usual

- When you have your period, you're in a lot of agony
- You bleed in between periods
- After using tampons, you have a sudden and severe nausea
- When your menstruation is excessively late and you are sexually active

It's understandable that discussing intimate details about your body can make you uncomfortable, but it can be helpful to set the record straight regarding menstruation. So let's bust some myths about periods, shall we?

Period myths and realities

It's always "that time of the month"

To begin, know that a period is not the same thing as a woman's menstrual cycle. The period refers to the time during which a woman actually bleeds, while the menstrual cycle encompasses the full time between the onset of one period and the onset of the next.

As previously mentioned, the typical length of a woman's menstrual cycle is 28 days, yet this is a number that has been extensively misrepresented. It's possible for a woman's period to be disrupted by things like travel, changes in weight, stress and emotional states, and medicines.

Therefore, it is not appropriate to make jokes about how women are "always on their period" or it always being "that time of the month." Just like every girl and woman is different, so is her monthly bleed, and a girl or woman's emotional responses to every day life situations should not be commented on in relation to her period.

Contrary to popular belief, period pain is not "just like" anything else you've felt

Yes, menstrual cramps do exist. We aren't talking about being hurt by stumbling into furniture here! Cramps can be so severe and disruptive to a woman's life that some may need to stay home from work and huddle in bed until the excruciating cramps eventually go away. This information is not presented to scare you, simply to let you know that this is a possible effect. Not all girls and women have severe cramps, but many do.

Dysmenorrhea is the official medical term for these cramps. According to studies, almost 20% of women suffer from severe dysmenorrhea that causes significant disruption to their lives. Lack of focus, increased anxiety, and irritability are all symptoms of this disorder.

You're just being moody

At this time, a woman's body goes through a real and noticeable transformation. When a woman is "PMSing," or having symptoms of premenstrual syndrome, her estrogen levels drop drastically and her progesterone levels rise dramatically in the days before the start of her menstruation.

The "happy hormone" serotonin is connected to estrogen, whereas progesterone is linked to the area of the brain that processes anxiety, despair, and fear. Hormonal fluctuations can cause a wide range of feelings, and while progesterone may dampen some of them, it also acts as a mood stabilizer.

It's easy to dismiss extreme shifts in mood as "simply hormones," but hormonal fluctuations really exist. It may be more frequent for women and girls, on a monthly basis, but that doesn't make these emotions any less real.

Women are ruled by hormones

When discussing women and girls, the term "hormonal" has been used to describe and diminish their mood swings and other symptoms. Some have even used the medical term of "hysteria" to describe women's emotions and actions, but here's a news flash: everyone has hormones, and no one enjoys it when theirs are played with. Yes, even men!

Take, for example, a trial on male contraception, which was terminated because the subjects were unable to tolerate the side effects of the contraceptive, which included acne, the discomfort of injections, and emotional issues. Imagine going through something similar every month! That's the reality of menstruation.

Period blood and its associated smells are gross

Having your period is not the body's way of rejecting fluids or of getting rid of poisons. It is a natural process containing some germs, uterine tissue, mucus, and blood. Along with your period you may experience some odors, which are also a natural part of the process, and neither the bleeding, nor the accompanying smells are anything to be ashamed of. There is nothing gross or disgusting about experiencing your period and everything that comes along with it.

Flowing blood in the veins is substantially different from period blood. Actually, did you know that period blood has been diluted? It's lacking in the number of cells found in non-period blood.

Periods are something to be ashamed of

It's past time for us as a society to get over the idea that menstruation is something to be embarrassed about and cleaned up as quickly as possible. However, the reality is that we have a considerable amount of shame to shed when it comes to periods.

No one should make you feel awkward or ashamed for needing a tampon or carrying a pad in your bag or in your pocket. In the same way that discussing periods shouldn't be out of the norm, neither are periods themselves. Let's break the cycle of shame and stigma. Periods are a natural biological response and nobody should be shamed for talking about or experiencing them.

What happens before, during and after your period

In case you've forgotten everything you learned in junior high health class, here's the deal: there's a scientific explanation for why your period ends and you drop weight: your body is actually shedding water. The explanations, in all honesty, are really interesting. Read this simple guide to all your period symptoms if you've ever wondered why you're feeling blue for no apparent reason or what's causing those zits on your chin. Taking care of yourself becomes a breeze with increased awareness of your own body, so read on!

It's important to keep in mind that menstrual symptoms might vary for each person, so the cycle below is to give you a general sense of what to expect. Use this as a starting point, but if you're suffering pain or irregularity, or if you're just curious and have more questions, consult your doctor.

The First Seven Days

Your period has arrived, and because of it, your levels of the female hormones estrogen and progesterone are at their lowest for the month. High levels of prostaglandin are floating around in your blood when your body removes blood and tissue from the uterine lining.

How you'll feel

Not so great, unfortunately! Prostaglandins in your bloodstream are the root of many unpleasant experiences: Your blood vessels tighten and your uterus contracts, resulting in cramping. The results of this can include nausea, vomiting, and diarrhea.

How to deal with it

You should consider taking ibuprofen (brand names include Advil and Motrin). Follow the dosage on the bottle and take with plenty of water as soon as symptoms are felt. Try lying down for anywhere from a few minutes to half an hour to allow the pain to subside. Keep drinking water throughout the day so that you can think more clearly and function more smoothly. As an additional comfort, warming packs and hot water bottles can be very reassuring and help soothe cramping.

Days 7 to 13

Put aside the pads and tampons till next time you have your period. You're seeing a rise in estrogen just as your uterus is beginning to re-line itself. At the same time, the egg inside the follicle continues to develop.

How you'll feel

Pretty good!

How to deal with it

Enjoy!

Days 14 to 20

It is now the phase of ovulation, which indicates that your estrogen levels have reached their highest point and that the egg has been released from the follicle into the fallopian tube (during each cycle, only one egg is produced). The uterine lining thickens as the egg travels down the fallopian tube. At this point, a sperm will arrive and possibly join with an egg, and the resulting embryo will require this sturdy surface to firmly connect to.

How you'll feel

When progesterone levels rise during ovulation, it can have a negative impact on your mood, appearance, and general wellbeing. In addition to gas and irritability, it can cause breakouts by increasing oil production and blocking pores.

How to deal with it

Currently, things are probably not going swimmingly in terms of how you are feeling. The best advice for this time of the month probably runs opposite to your natural inclinations: move your body. In order to minimize bloating, you should aim to exercise a little bit daily and cut out on salty foods. The release of endorphins during exercise has been shown to have a calming effect on emotions, which should make you feel better overall.

Days 21 to 25

The uterus will expel its excess lining and hormone levels will drop unless a sperm successfully joins an egg and begins maturing into a fetus (i.e., you're pregnant).

How you'll feel

You've had to deal with the ups and downs of the past few days, and now you're probably also suffering from weariness, hunger, distraction, and additional bloating. It's not great, but it's a clue that your period is approaching, and it's very neat to be able to interpret your body's signals like that!

How to deal with it

Take care of yourself, get plenty of sleep, and maintain your exercise routine to maintain a healthy equilibrium. Getting your recommended daily allowance of calcium is beneficial for your health in general, but there is some evidence to suggest it may also play a role in improving your mood.

Days 26 to 30

While your hormone levels are down, your period will begin.

How you'll feel

You may notice some extra bloating, breast soreness, and intermittent cramping in the days leading up to your period, as your cycle nears its finish and the start of a new one nears.

How to deal with it

Do not be scared to take some ibuprofen a few days before your period starts if you know you will experience severe cramping. Preventing discomfort is less difficult than trying to alleviate it once it has set in.

How to care for your body and mind during your period

It can be difficult to make sense of our menstrual cycles. This may be especially true for young girls just learning for the first time how this whole process works. However, all girls and women may better understand how to care for ourselves throughout the entire menstrual cycle if we educate ourselves about our bodies and their unique requirements, not just during flow. Here are some things you can do to care for your mind and body during each stage of your monthly cycle.

The first seven days

Your menstrual cycle begins the week of your period (days 1 - 7). The uterine lining is shed during menstruation. This lining was developed to protect the uterus in case of pregnancy. A lot of "out with the old, in with the new" is happening at this period, both in your mind and body.

For physical relief

You can get instant comfort from a heating pad, which will help ease your pain. Remember to breathe when you meditate (if you don't already, now is a good time to start!) and take long walks. Nourish your body by eating more healthy fats, lean proteins, dark leafy greens, and dark chocolate. To relax and restore balance, sip on some hot herbal tea. Sleep if you need to, rest if you need to. Be gentle with yourself and listen to the cues your body is giving you.

For mental health

The onset of menstruation can be a little more difficult to deal with for those who suffer from a more drawn-out case of Premenstrual Syndrome (PMS), which can cause feelings of brain fog, irritability, and fatigue. A rise in estrogen and "feel-good hormones" may give some people a noticeable boost in energy on the first day of blood flow. As you near the end of your period (days 5–7), you may experience a heightened sense of connection to the world. This is due to the deficient amounts of progesterone.

Spend time thinking deeply, creating, or talking to friends and family. Pay attention to what your physical and emotional needs are during this time; you may want some additional rest, or you may feel the desire to be out and about and connect with others.

2nd week

As your body becomes ready to release an egg, endometrial lining repairs begin. The levels of estrogen and testosterone in your body are also increasing.

For physical relief

During this time you will begin to feel more like your true self, and because your body has probably shed some water weight that it was using to keep you going throughout your period, you may be feeling less puffy than usual. To top it all off, your skin is probably clearer of any hormonal acne.

Since you will likely be feeling more energetic, this is a great time to be social or active. Allow for additional movement and exercise, but don't push yourself too much. Balance your need for hydration, rest and getting things done.

For mental health

You have a greater sense of mental vitality and self-assurance. Redirect your energies. Free up some time for making things or completing tasks. Avoid over-stressing yourself and remember to take regular, conscious breaths because an increase in estrogen might produce an abundance of energy.

Third week

This is the most fertile period of the month, meaning that there is a higher risk of pregnancy during this time.

For physical relief

Egg release occurs on only one of the five to seven days during this phase. When an egg is discharged into the fallopian tubes, many people experience cramping in their ovaries (either on the right or left). The egg waits for a sperm for a full day. If and egg is not fertilized, it naturally disintegrates.

Since this is the most fertile period in which to get pregnant, most people experience a surge in desire at this time. Additionally, other people's pheromones may arouse your interest. Scented candles and aromatic oils are especially relaxing now.

For mental health

It's a good idea to keep track of where you are in your cycle, whether you're just starting or finishing ovulation. Honor your mind and body and do what makes you feel the best.

Keep in mind that increasing progesterone levels could cause a decrease in desire as you near the end of ovulation. This may lead to decreased vitality. Premenstrual syndrome (PMS) refers to the fluctuating emotions some may experience before their period actually begins. Keep in mind that your body is undergoing a lot of changes at the moment, and now is a good time to treat it gently.

Fourth week

Boosted progesterone levels after ovulation help the uterine lining thicken, making a suitable environment for an embryo to implant. In the absence of a fertilized egg, your levels of estrogen, testosterone, and progesterone will drop, which can have serious effects on how you feel.

For physical relief

A renewed surge in libido occurs around this time, which may help alleviate some of the unpleasant feelings you may be experiencing. Hormonal fluctuations might manifest physically as acne breakouts, breast soreness, and a general lack of energy.

Get lots of shut-eye and try not to overbook yourself socially. Maintaining a balanced diet and regular exercise will help stabilize your mood and ease any aches and pains you might be experiencing during the week.

For mental health

Tell those close to you what's going on so you can feel less isolated. Just know that this is a normal part of your body's process of renewal. Spend some time alone doing things like reading and writing. Repeating words of affirmation such as "I love you, body" as often as possible can help you feel better. If you want to maintain an optimistic frame of mind, try keeping a gratitude journal before bed.

If you're feeling down, talk to someone you trust or see a therapist trained to work with teens.

During the more challenging phases of our cycles, we likely would appreciate some quiet time to recharge. Many of us, however, have hectic schedules and it can be hard to find time to stop what we're doing to sit down and write in a notebook or soak in a hot tub, but we should try to make time to care for ourselves as best we can. Our minds and bodies will thank us! Period shame is still common, which is why it's crucial that we have open conversations about our periods, our cycles and what's going on with us physically, neatly and emotionally during all of this in order to help end the taboo surrounding it.

5. Social Changes

The physical and mental development of a teen is accompanied by significant shifts in their interactions with members of their family and their circle of friends. During puberty, there is frequently a reordering of family relationships. Teens typically express a desire for increased autonomy and greater psychological separation from their parents.

Changes in relationships and friendships during puberty and teen years, and how to handle these

The importance of social relationships and friendships typically comes to the foreground for a teen. This comprises friends of the same gender, as well as groups of friends of different genders. When a person reaches a certain age, they tend to naturally become more interested in dating and sexual interactions.

Changes to one's relationship with oneself

A fresh awareness of one's own identity typically emerges somewhere during the teen years. This may include shifts in the following aspects of one's self-understanding:

Independence

This implies being responsible for one's own choices and conclusions, as well as acting in accordance with one's own internal deliberations and evaluations. Teenagers begin to acquire the skills necessary to solve difficulties on their own.

As teenagers become more capable of reasoning and intuition, they also begin to take on increasingly complex duties. They eventually begin to take pleasure and gain more confidence in their own ideas and actions. Additionally, teens begin to speculate and daydream about their future and adulthood as this stage of life progresses.

Identity

This refers to an individual's self-awareness or their sense of self - who they understand themselves to be. The development of a secure sense of one's own identity and a personal identity is among the most important goals of the adolescent years.

Teens start to become capable of using their own discretion and coming to their own conclusions. Teenagers confront their own difficulties and begin to form a concept of who they are as they go along with the progression of life's events. When a teen is unable to come to terms with who they are in terms of their body, their sexuality, and their level of independence, they may have difficulty forming a distinct and secure concept of themselves or their identity.

Self-esteem

How much one appreciates oneself is a measure of that person's self-esteem. At the beginning of adolescence, it is not uncommon for a person's self-esteem to begin to decline. This happens as a result of the numerous changes that take place within the body, as well as the introduction of new views and perspectives on various topics. As they develop, teenagers will begin to have a deeper understanding of themselves, as well as of the people they aspire to become.

They become aware of the discrepancies that exist between the way they behave and the way they believe they should behave. When teens begin to reflect on their behaviors and qualities, they are forced to confront how they value and evaluate themselves. A significant number of teens place a high value on their appearance, as well as the way they appear to others. Low self-esteem is a common result in adolescents who have negative perceptions of their own attractiveness. Teenagers typically experience a rise in self-esteem as they mature and gain a more accurate idea of who they are.

Changes in the connections between peers

More time is spent with friends during the teenage years. Teens report that their friends have made them feel more understood and accepted than their parents or other family members. As a result, the amount of time spent with one's parents and other members of the family continues to decrease during this time.

Teenagers who share similar interests, social class, and ethnic backgrounds are more likely to form close friendships with one another. Friendships formed in childhood are typically based on activities that are done together, while friendships formed during adolescence grow to include people who have similar perspectives, values, activities and interests. Educational pursuits are also frequently a common ground for the formation of friendships among teens.

Personal, in-depth, and self-revealing conversations with close friends are beneficial for exploring identities and defining one's sense of self. Teenagers can learn more about their sexuality and how they feel about it by having essential conversations within these important friendships. The friendships of teenage boys are typically less close and personal than those of teenage girls. Boys are more inclined to surround themselves with peers who emphasize affirming each other's value through deeds rather than through words, as tends to be the case with girls.

Changes in relationship: from platonic to romantic

Both sexual curiosity and societal and cultural norms and expectations play a role in the evolution of romantic pairings between people. It is via experience and observation that one is able to learn the social and cultural norms and expectations that pertain to sexual relationships. The struggle to gain control over sexual and aggressive urges is one of the developmental tasks that must be completed during adolescence.

Impulsive sexual activity, a diverse spectrum of experimental relationships characterized by mutual exploration, and finally, intercourse are all examples of sexual activities that sometimes occur during adolescence. Both biological differences, and disparities in the ways in which males and females are socialized to interact with one another contribute to distinct expectations of what they should get out of romantic and sexual relationships.

These factors have the potential to affect sexual experiences and can have repercussions on subsequent sexual behavior and partnerships. With the passage of time and through understanding themselves and their partners, a loving couple might eventually develop a sexual partnership that is satisfying for both partners.

Social changes

When a person reaches puberty, their connections with their family and friends, as well as the beginnings of new types of interactions, can shift.

Friends

Friends are people with whom you can have meaningful conversations and openly discuss your thoughts, emotions, and experiences. Friends are people who, even when you disagree with them or desire to spend some time apart for a bit, nonetheless manage to make your time spent with them a positive experience overall. During puberty, your friendships will go through some transition, some minor, some major.

As your hobbies and interests evolve, you might find that you start to connect with new people. It's possible that you have one best buddy, or even several best friends right now. It's wonderful to have special individuals in your life who are close to you, but it's essential that the friendships you have don't prevent you from getting to know new people or being authentically you. It's possible that you'll need to adjust the amount of time you spend with a specific friend in order to make room in your life for the companionship of others. It is also acceptable, and even a healthy and good idea for you to spend time by yourself.

Attraction

It's possible that during puberty you'll feel an attraction to a certain person or even to several different people. To be attracted to someone means to have romantic or sexual desire when in the company of that person or to like them more than a friend.

You might find someone of the opposite sex attractive, someone of the same sex attractive, or both sexes attractive. On the other hand, you might not find anyone attractive at all. Nobody has the right to make fun of or bully someone else due to the fact that they are attracted to another person or not attracted to anybody at all, as all of these forms of attraction are considered to be healthy, natural and valid.

New relationships

There are occasions when you might find yourself becoming attracted to a particular someone. It's possible that you have romantic feelings whenever you think about them and that you want to spend more time with them. There are moments when that individual will share your feelings, but there are also occasions when they won't. At first, it may be challenging to cope with this situation, because you may feel rejected. Nonetheless, it is important to keep in mind that you are a one-of-a-kind individual who possesses many admirable features, and while this one person may not be the right one for you, that does not mean there is nobody with whom you will find a romantic connection. It's also important to respect the way others feel, and not try to force them to feel the same way you do.

When two people feel attracted to one another, they have the option of moving their relationship to a more intimate level. The dynamics of your connection are entirely up to you. Both parties need to have a conversation about how they are feeling, what they want from the relationship, and what types of things they are interested in doing together. It's important to be on the same page and respect each others' boundaries and feelings.

Intimate connections can be very precious, but a healthy relationship doesn't interfere with the other important relationships in your life, like the ones you have with your friends and family, nor should they interfere with your goals and aspirations for your life. If you discover that you are unable to maintain other connections due to a lack of time, you might want to consider how you might better distribute your time among the various relationships in your life.

Do you want to...?

It is essential for the success of any relationship that both parties involved feel at ease and only engage in activities that they choose for themselves. Because of this, you should always ask someone's permission before kissing or touching them in any way. This is what is referred to as obtaining "consent."

Try asking some of these questions:
- Are you comfortable?
- Do you want to keep going?
- Do you want to stop?
- How do you feel right now?

Also, make sure that your romantic partner is aware of how you are feeling, as well as the things that you enjoy and dislike.

What happens if you don't want to...?

If you don't want to, you are under no obligation to touch or kiss another person, nor should you feel pressured to allow them to touch or kiss you. Even if the person touching you is someone you like, you have the right at any time to tell them to stop if they are touching you in a way that makes you uncomfortable. It is crucial to alert a responsible adult if you are made to feel uncomfortable by another person.

Qualities of healthy relationships: trust, communication, boundaries, respect!

Adolescence is a time when young people learn how to build secure and healthy connections with their friends, parents, caregivers, teachers and romantic partners, among other important individuals in their lives. Teenagers frequently experiment with assuming a variety of personas and roles, and the various connections they have at this stage of development all contribute to the building of their identities.

During adolescence, one's peers, in particular, have a significant impact on the development of one's identity. Relationships with caring adults, such as parents or other caregivers, mentors, or coaches, however, serve as the foundation for all other types of interactions and serve as models for how a young person should behave in such relationships.

In a broader sense, healthy relationships for teenagers are ones in which they are able to securely feel and exhibit respect for both themselves and others. This is typically the result of both parties having trust in one another, being honest, having good communication, being understanding and calm throughout conflicts, and consenting to do something.

Unhealthy relationships, on the other hand, typically have an imbalance of power (for instance, there is no consent, mutual trust, compromise, or honesty), and either one or both of the people involved in the relationship may struggle to communicate effectively or keep their anger in check. Some relationships such as these eventually turn violent on some level, whether it is physically, emotionally, or sexually.

In the beginning phases of a romantic partnership, it is natural for both partners to view the world through a rosier lens than later on down the road. But for some, those rose-colored glasses become blinders, preventing them from seeing the signs that their relationship is unhealthy. Read on to learn about some of the things to look out for in a healthy relationship.

What are some characteristics of a healthy relationship?

If you're in a committed relationship, I hope you're being respectful to one another. Do you have any doubts about this being the case? Put the heady rush of newfound passion on hold for a moment and assess whether or not your relationship possesses the following traits:

Mutual respect

Does your partner understand how amazing you are and why you're so special? Make sure that they like you for the person you are. Does this person take your concerns seriously when you tell them you don't feel comfortable doing something, and then immediately back off? Are they interested in your life and concerned about your wellbeing? When two people have respect for one another, it indicates that they care about one another, that they comprehend one another's limits, and that they would never test those limits.

Trust

Your boyfriend walks into the room as you are having a conversation with a guy from your French class. Does he lose all composure, or does he continue going because he is confident in your relationship and trusts you? Jealousy is a normal human emotion, therefore there's actually nothing wrong with feeling it every once in a while. But what's really important is how a person responds when they have feelings of jealousy or envy. Do they respond in destructive or harmful ways? If you don't trust each other, it will be impossible for you to have a happy and healthy relationship.

Honesty

Honesty is closely related to the concept of trust since it is difficult to have faith in another person when you yourself are not being truthful. Have you ever uncovered a significant lie told by your partner? What if they lied to you and said they had to work on Friday night, but it turned out that they were actually out with other pals watching a movie? You will have a much harder time trusting them the next time they tell you that they need to work, and your faith in them will be on fragile ground as a result. Honesty is important, but be gentle with your words and actions, and take into account your partner's feelings when you are being honest with them. Even when the truth may hurt, there are ways to deliver the message without adding insult to injury.

Support

Your partner should be there for you when you need them, in the good times and the bad. Some individuals are wonderful to have around when everything in your life seems to be coming apart, but they aren't all that interested in hearing about the good things that are happening in your life. In a healthy relationship, your significant other should be there to comfort you when you receive bad news, and they should be there to celebrate with you when you earn the main role in a school play, for example.

Fairness and equality

In order for your relationship to work, there needs to be give and take. Do you take turns deciding which of the newest movies you should watch? Do you and your significant other spend as much time with their friends as you do with your own? When one person in a relationship always tries to get their way, or frequently behave in ways that override the needs and desires of their partner, the dynamic quickly deteriorates into a power struggle, and things go from bad to worse very quickly.

Separate identities

In order for a relationship to be strong and healthy, both parties need to be willing to make concessions. However, this does not mean that you should feel as though you are losing touch with who you are as a person. Both of you had your own life (family, friends, interests, hobbies, etc.) before you started dating, and that shouldn't change now that you're in a relationship together.

You shouldn't have to act as though you enjoy something that you don't, stop hanging out with the people you care about, or stop participating in the things that bring you joy. In addition, you shouldn't be afraid to keep exploring and developing your skills and interests, meeting new people, and making progress in your life. A healthy relationship allows for all this to continue to happen for both partners.

Strong communication

Are you able to communicate with one another and discuss your feelings, as well as things that are significant to you? Don't bottle up your emotions out of fear that they won't be received well by your partner or by your close friends and family. And if you need some space to think about something before you are ready to talk about it, a good partner will the will give you that space so that you may do that thinking before you bring it up.

Mutual empathy

Empathy is an additional crucial characteristic of a healthy connection. Having empathy for someone means making an effort to understand how they are feeling, and attempting to see things from their perspective. Being able to listen to and empathize with your partner's concerns and difficulties is more important than ignoring them in order to actively attempt to find solutions to those issues. If you pay more attention and try to see things from their side, you will find that you get closer to them rather than further apart, which will then allow you to find solutions to any issues together.

Kindness

Give your partner the same level of care and attention that you would like to receive. Consider the ways in which they could use your assistance, and try to be considerate of their needs and concerns. Being considerate, thoughtful, kind, and respectful to one another is an important part of maintaining successful relationships.

Boundaries

It is essential that you do not lose sight of the fact that the two of you are distinct individuals with your own needs and requirements, some of which you may or may not share. You are not going to see eye-to-eye on everything, and you might not even want the same things at times. It is imperative that these distinctions be respected, and that individuals not push the boundaries of one another in any way, shape, or form. This applies to both emotional and physical boundaries, as well as any other forms of boundaries. Having clear boundaries, and respecting them are essential components of any healthy connection.

Relationships have the potential to be a source of joy, romance, and excitement as well as powerful sentiments and, on occasion, sadness. It's important to keep in mind that it's healthy to be selective about the people you let into your life, whether you're currently in a relationship or not.

Familial relationships

Teenagers face a number of issues as they find themselves and grow into young adults, and their shifting sense of self and their social role can affect their relationships with parents and siblings, as they may be tempted to reject family during this trying time. Instead of progressively becoming more autonomous as they age, teens may feel pressured to suddenly become self-sufficient and immediately figure out everything on their own.

Even though they know their parents would rush to their aid in a crisis, in their search for independence, teenagers are more likely to seek space and solitude than to call out to them for help. Adolescence is a time of transition for families, as parents attempt to strike a balance between encouraging their child's growing independence and keeping them safe from harm. For many households, arguments between parents and children are a common problem.

The rejection of childhood

Adolescence is a time when boundaries between family members tend to blur. Many teens equate maturing with losing their innocence, and as they mature into independent thinkers with greater responsibilities, it's natural for them to distance themselves from others who still treat them like children, this includes their parents, who may have a hard time viewing them as independent, maturing individuals.

Some teens attempt to distance themselves from their younger selves by engaging in dangerous adult actions that they believe will fast-track them to being considered "mature." For others, the search for independence comes from engaging less with their parents and displaying less public affection or not checking in as regularly.

Changes in personality during teen years

Many factors contribute to teens' emotional and behavioral challenges during adolescence, but everyone reacts to the change from childhood to adulthood in their own unique way. Many teenagers go through a series of changes throughout this time of growth, which can feel like a major upheaval and cause strain on family connections. Some of these changes include:

- Becoming more argumentative
- Increased sadness and irritation
- Being less compliant and more defiant
- Being less extroverted and more reclusive
- Being less empathic and more concerned with one's own welfare
- Becoming less grateful and appreciative
- Being more disorganized and less orderly

- Spending less time with family and more with friends and peers

Parent-child disputes

Even though most kids don't reveal all the specifics, teens nonetheless evaluate their own family ties in light of what they've heard about their peers' families. During this stage of a teen's life, most arguments between parents and their teens are not caused by a hostile household, but by a failure to communicate effectively. Misunderstandings are rampant, as parents find it hard to view the world through the eyes of their teen, and teens don't have the experience yet to view the world from the perspective of an adult.

As kids get older, they also tend to push their parents' buttons more often. This is a regular occurrence amongst teens, and can cause a lot of worry for both parents and young people. When both parties look back on happier times in the past, they may wonder what changed. Parents may seem unreasonable, authoritarian, and harsh to their teens. And parents may wonder where their children, who were once helpful and responsive and are now reckless and dismissive, have disappeared to. These points of view often feed off of each other, making both sides even more confused. During this time, many families report less emotional intimacy between the parent and teen generations.

More common than disagreements over religion and morality are those over dress, music, and hobbies. While some teens may engage in them, drinking, drug use and criminal behavior are not typical causes of family conflict. Despite this, it is estimated that intense, ongoing and unhealthy conflict occurs between parents and teenagers in over 5 million American households, which accounts for approximately 20 percent of all families in the country.

Extreme forms of this stressful environment have been linked to a variety of undesirable consequences, such as teen delinquency, running away from home, increased rates of school dropout, unintended pregnancies, and substance misuse. Teen conflict often rises in the first few years of puberty, peaks between 14 and 16 years old, and then reduces in the later years of adolescence (ages 17-18).

The transition from childhood to adulthood is marked by several changes, some of which might strain the parent-teen relationship. Teenagers' enhanced reasoning skills prompt them to demand explanations for practices they had previously taken at face value, as well as the opportunity to present opposing viewpoints. Because of their growing capacity for independent thought, they are less inclined to follow parental orders, requests or advice than they once were.

They may become more critical of their parents' decisions and actions as they gain intellectual maturity and develop a strong sense of idealism.

As they age, teenagers no longer view their parents as the final arbiters of right and wrong. They begin to develop their own unique perspectives while also learning to appreciate the value of those other than their parents. In addition, with hormones running amok, teens may overreact to even the most offhand comment from their parents.

With the tremendous shifts that occur between puberty and adolescence, it can be hard for parents to make sense of the change in their child's behavior. Teenagers, who may have been docile in the past, may become less eager to cooperate if they are not given an explanation they find convincing.

Teens' resistance and opposition may be misunderstood by their parents, who see that their kids are acting differently than they did in late childhood. In turn, parents may demand more compliance in response to what they perceive as the teen's lack of it, which the teen may interpret as a decrease in their own freedom at precisely the time when they desire greater independence.

Fostering wholesome family ties

Despite the major ups and downs teens and their parents are going through, there are ways to get through this time and strengthen familial relationships. Let's take a look at what some these can look like.

Affection and gratitude

When things are most challenging, take some time out to remind each other how much you value and cherish one another. Simply telling your loved ones that you value them and your bond, or expressing this through a hug or even a comforting smile, will go a long way toward bridging divides.

Sharing a dinner together as a family

Every member of the family should make an effort to sit down together for a meal at least once a day. It's easier to get people to open up and share their thoughts if they're not made to feel like they have to, so don't force anyone to express what they don't want or aren't ready to. Perhaps they might tomorrow! Leave your devices out of it (TV, phones) and focus on each other and the nice meal in front of you.

Family outings

As uncool as you may think this is as a teen, try to make time for family outings. The bonding power of a weekend getaway with the family is not to be underestimated. It can bring you closer together and give you a chance to catch up with what's going on in everyone's busy lives.

One-on-one time

Spend time alone with your parents. Talk to them and you might be surprised by how much they actually understand and empathize with what you are going through. After all, they were once teens too! They might just need some time to remember what that felt like, and hearing from you about your thoughts and struggles can help jog their memory, allowing them to give you some good advice since believe it or not, they've probably learned a thing or two since then! Doing something together regularly, such as taking a stroll, watching a movie, or sharing a story, might help bring you closer together and give you a better understanding of one another.

Help out around the house

Kids and teens who have chores they help out with at home feel that they have a meaningful role to play in the family's daily life. Chores, grocery shopping, and assisting family members of all ages are all examples of things you can do around the house and ways you can have a say in how your household is run.

Respect the rules

Teenagers benefit from the stability, structure, and predictability provided by mutually agreed upon rules, limitations, and penalties. You may have an impulse to break the rules, but try to remember that these weren't created to hurt you. If there are rules in the house that you think are unfair, talk to your parents or guardian and see if you can come to an agreement that works for all of you.

Family meetings

It often helps to talk things out as a family. Regular family meetings, or check-ins can ensure that everyone's voices are heard and that all members of the family have a hand in crafting a resolution to any issues that come up.

Making and keeping friends

Friendship growth includes making new friends, maintaining existing friendships, and letting old ones go as we mature. When children are young, parents often act as friendship matchmakers, setting up play dates between their kids and other kids. Though parents may worry about the effect of their children's friends on them, the reality is that teens are in control of their own friendships. Teens are still developing into fully formed adults, so it's important to let them handle their own friendships while providing support and guidance from the wings.

While teens should ultimately make all friendship-related decisions on their own, there are ways parents can help guide and influence those decisions toward making healthy connections. Parents should have open discussions with their teenagers on the characteristics of positive friends. Defining what a teen should expect from their friends and what true friendship consists of will allow teens to more easily know how to spot a good friend.

What makes a true friend?

Honesty

The truth is what makes a good friend. Though they may not divulge every personal detail, their goals are made crystal clear. They are honest with you about who they are and what's going on, and they'll let you know if something doesn't feel quite right. Good friends are honest, but not brutally so. They know how to tell you the truth while being gentle.

Common interests

Friendships flourish when people share common interests, and it's possible that you'll pick your pals based on how fascinating they seem. While common interests bring you together, you might also find that your differences keep things interesting! You should have enough of both in a friendship to allow for a connection that grows over time.

Attentive

A true friend takes the time to hear you out and observes your unique qualities. They will be pay attention to and be considerate of your needs and feelings, which will help build trust in your friendship.

Supportive

A supportive friend helps you grow. When you're in the presence of this person, you can't help but feel good about yourself because they know exactly how to bring out the best in you. They won't force you to alter who you are or put you in circumstances where you might feel unsafe or lose yourself. However, a true friend knows that being supportive doesn't mean accepting any kind of behaviour, especially if it is destructive. They will know and not be afraid to tell you when you are wrong, and a strong friendship will not be broken by them telling you this.

Trustworthy

A loyal friend won't slander you behind your back, try to ruin your good name, or take credit for your accomplishments or success at school, work or in life. If you ever find yourself in trouble or in need of help, you know you can call them and they'll be there. You can trust them with your innermost thoughts and secrets, and openly share your hopes and dreams with them.

Compassionate

Good friends are concerned about you. They care about your wellbeing, and your life in general. This care and compassion may look different depending on the friend, but there's no mistaking it when you feel it. Knowing that someone is interested in what's going on in your life is a good indicator that they care about you.

Accepting

Friends who truly care about you accept you as you are and don't try to change you. As you develop and grow into yourself, they are flexible and accepting of your flaws and the changes you're going through and they don't judge you or your actions.

Forgiving

Nobody is perfect, and because of this fact, we are all capable of causing each other pain. However, true friends are able to build a strong foundation of friendship based on all of the characteristics mentioned earlier, which will allow them to make amends and go on with the friendship when things go wrong.

When a friendship has gone bad

Unfortunately, at some point in your life you may end up in a friendship that has gone wrong. A harmful friend is one who gossips about someone behind their back, criticizes them constantly, discourages them from making new friends, refuses to negotiate during arguments, or is a bad influence and gets you into trouble.

If you find yourself in this kind of friendship, please know that you always have the option to leave it behind. While it may be difficult to terminate a harmful connection, staying in an abusive friendship is much more distressing. The best way to end a friendship with someone is on good terms, but this is not always possible. Read on for some things to look out for to identify whether your friendship is unhealthy.

Warning signs of a unhealthy friendship

Sometimes, relationships between friends can become unhealthy over time. Feelings of low self-esteem, anxiety, tension, and exhaustion can all be the result of being in a toxic friendship. It can be tough for teenagers to let go of a close friend, because they are unable to spot the signs, or because they are afraid of ending things, so they may keep a friendship going for longer than they should.

However, if warning signs are ignored, the relationship may have already sustained significant damage. It's crucial to recognize the indications that it's time to end a friendship, even if it seemed to be a good one for a long time.

Drama, drama, drama!

Relationships with friends should not be taxing or draining. If your relationship with your friend is constantly fraught with tension and drama, you should probably cut ties.

Control

It's a red flag that your friend isn't supportive of your growth as an individual and a member of society if they try to control who you spend time with, and express jealousy when you spend time with others. A true friend will have no issue with you making new friends and connections, because they know your relationship is secure and because they are happy to see you spread your wings and fly.

Endless fights

We know, the tumultuous years of middle and high school are fertile ground for drama! Some fights with your greatest friends are normal, because you are all going through big changes and this can weigh on you, but it's not a good sign if your pal is consistently angry with you or overreacts frequently for no reason. For a friendship to thrive, you must be able to open up to one another and trust one another, even when tensions arise.

Breaking boundaries

Good friends are those who stand by you even if your own boundaries are different from their own. It's time to part ways if your friend is constantly pushing you to do things that make you uncomfortable or that they know would get you in hot water. If they don't respect your boundaries, it's time to cut them loose.

They're being unkind to you

Friends should always be honest with one another, but there's a fine line between being truthful and being hurtful when bringing up uncomfortable topics. Friends who mock you, insult you, or say unpleasant things while passing them off as "jokes" are not friends worth retaining.

They are cruel

Everyone gets angry or frustrated once in a while, but if you witness your friend being cruel to you or anybody else, for example, if they seek to mock, embarrass or humiliate others - especially more than once - it's perhaps time to reevaluate whether this is a person you want to remain friends with.

What are some ways to cut ties with a toxic pal?

Suppose you and your best friend are currently experiencing some major warning signs. What do you do? You can break off a friendship or put some space between you and a friend without hurting anyone's feelings or causing unnecessary tension by following a few simple guidelines.

Separate yourself from the group

Gently at first, then more and more frequently, start declining social invitations and activities with them. Put that distance between you and your toxic friend to good use by starting to seek out other, more positive social interactions. As opposed to adding more drama with a sudden stop, you can accomplish this very gradually.

Establish both mental and physical limits

You can put more physical space between the two of you by rearranging your schedule so you see them less - maybe by moving to a different seat in class, or avoiding congested areas. Make room for yourself emotionally by avoiding their attempts to include you in conversations and not lingering in conversation. There is no need to be hostile, you can still remain civil while choosing to keep your distance.

Be more assertive

If you prefer to be more direct, there is nothing wrong with giving a friend an honest, yet kind explanation for why you've been withdrawing recently. It's healthy to communicate when your relationship with someone has changed. Mastering the ability to communicate openly and honestly in personal interactions is a skill that will serve you well throughout your entire life, despite the fact that doing so may at first make you feel uneasy.

If your friend confronts you about the rift in your relationship, it can sometimes better to be forthright about the situation. By practicing this talk in advance with a trustworthy adult, you can reduce your nervousness and avoid being frozen in the moment, or you can be ready to initiate the conversation yourself if you prefer.

6. Self-esteem and body image

Possessing a healthy dose of self-assurance is helpful for successfully navigating your teen years, although it's frequently a struggle. Having faith in yourself - this is what it is to be self-confident. Possessing a healthy sense of one's own value and worth is the essence of having good self-esteem. Teens that have a lot of faith in themselves are those who are confident in their own intelligence, abilities, and knowledge. You are less inclined to give in to peer pressure and more likely to pursue your own objectives and dreams if you have good self-esteem. Being socially savvy and able to weather the natural storms of adolescence are two additional benefits of being a self-assured teen. But there's more to the picture! Let's explore this further below.

What are the sources of self-esteem?

Parents, educators, and other parties

The individuals around us have the power to shape our sense of self-worth. As a result of their positive reinforcement, we have a heightened sense of self-worth. By extending grace in the face of failure, others help us come to terms with our own humanity. Friends and harmonious relationships are key to experiencing a sense of belonging.

When you experience the contrary, where you are reprimanded more than praised by those in your life, it can be really tough to feel good about yourself. Negative interactions with other family members or your classmates can have a negative impact on your sense of worth. Abusive comments can leave lasting scars on one's psyche.

Internal thoughts and feelings

The way you talk to yourself also has a significant impact on your self-esteem. Your self-esteem will suffer if you continually have negative thoughts about yourself, such as "I'm such a loser" or "I'll never make friends." Try taking a different perspective. When the outcome isn't what you had hoped it would be, try saying "I didn't come out on top this time, but there will be other opportunities." Or "I'm capable of meeting new people and making new friends." The last two are more optimistic and affirm who you are rather than criticize you.

The harsh remarks of others might sometimes be the source of our own inner voice. Or it may come from the difficult moments we have had to endure in life. Sometimes it's just us being overly critical of ourselves when we hear that voice. However, the mental monologue is something we have control over. Improved self-esteem is a skill that can be developed, it just takes practice.

Skills to succeed

Learning something new, like a language, an art form, or a craft or skill, can make us happy. Try your hand at a sport, an instrument, or riding a bike. Make the bed, clean the car, do some other house chores to help out around the house. Lend a hand to someone, walk the dog for a friend or family member. There is always a reason to be proud of your accomplishments and your progress, and your desire to help others. Take a breath and survey your accomplishments. Go ahead and give yourself permission to enjoy them! Taking stock of this can help remind you that you are capable, and sometimes that's just the boost we need to feel better about ourselves.

Increase your sense of pride and accomplishment

Say goodbye to worry and dread

The inner critic who constantly tells us, "You're not good enough!" gradually quiets as we develop self-assurance. As our self-assurance improves, we begin to feel less dread and anxiety about what we can and cannot accomplish, because our belief in our own abilities grows. We no longer think "I can't do this" and instead begin to think "I've got this!"

Boost your follow-through

Sometimes our insecurity-based worries cause us to be frozen in fear, and leave us struggling to find the will to move forward. When we don't believe in ourselves, we always seem to find an excuse not to pursue our goals. As your self-assurance grows, you'll be less inhibited by your worries and more able to pursue your dreams and you will start following through on things you were unable to before.

Where you were once starting things and giving up due to beliefs that you couldn't succeed, you now will be seeing things all the way through, and with every new accomplishment, your self-belief will grow!

Accept defeat and setbacks

Everyone is guilty of being too hard on themselves when they inevitably make a mistake, but why? Consistency in one's own belief is key. We'll fare better against failure and setback if we have faith in ourselves. No matter who we are, or how accomplished, intelligent and capable we are, we will experience failures and challenges at some point in life. What's important is how we bounce back from these. When we have faith in ourselves, our ability to come back from these tough moments is much stronger.

Improve your relationships

People who believe in themselves are better able to support those around them. When we don't believe in ourselves, we obsess over what other people think. This makes it tough to invest in the lives of those around us as well as in ourselves.

People who are secure in themselves are also less likely to settle for unhealthy partners. If you work on boosting your confidence, you may find the strength to leave the relationships that cause you stress and misery and the courage to pursue the ones that will bring you joy.

Cultivate a deeper awareness of who you are

The ability to trust oneself is also essential for establishing one's values and principles. People who are secure in themselves are able to recognize the unique combination of qualities they possess, including their strengths and weaknesses. It will give you the confidence to advocate for your rights and those of others.

Despite the benefits of high self-esteem in teens, research suggests that as many as half of teenagers experience low self-esteem at some point during their development. An overwhelming number of factors—including, but not limited to, social media, unrealistic physical expectations, societal pressures, changing bodies, puberty, peer pressure, and hormones—contribute to reduced levels of confidence among teenagers. As a result, teens are more likely to experience negative emotions, psychological disorders, poor body image, and substance use.

There are a number of strategies teens can implement to begin to feel more confident:

Get your mind off the bad

Confident people have mastered self-love to the point where they can walk away from negative situations. Exercising self-love means distancing yourself from negative influences. It can be hard to identify these as you're still figuring yourself out, but chances are if something isn't sitting well with you, you will know - it may manifest physically, such as tension in your shoulders, or with a feeling of discomfort. When you're feeling this, try stepping away from the situation and seeing if you feel any better, both physically and mentally. The more you do this, the more you will be able to recognize a negative situation and whether you want to remove yourself from it.

Doing a digital detox

While it's true that social media has the potential to be amusing, it also has the capability of becoming really poisonous. Taking a vacation from social media may help if you feel overwhelmed by negative emotions or find yourself comparing your life to the perfectly staged images online. Put your efforts into things that bring you joy instead. Take some time to yourself by going for a stroll, reading a book, listening to music, or hanging out with loved ones.

End harmful relationships

Among the many ways to increase confidence, this may be one of the most demanding and rewarding. It may be time to reassess a friendship or romantic partnership with someone who continually puts you down or makes you feel inadequate. You should either reduce or entirely eliminate your interaction with these people. Relationships, whether platonic or romantic, should elevate and enrich one's life, rather than pull one down. Pay attention to your instinct, and if it doesn't lead you in the right direction, talk to a trusted adult or friend who might be able to give you a helpful outside perspective.

Quit bad routines

Of course, this is easier said than done. Do you find that you frequently engage in behavior that leaves you feeling ashamed of your actions or yourself? Whether it's drinking, or beating yourself up inside, what helps you break these habits?

You need to make an effort to avoid returning to that behavior. A good dose of inspiration may be necessary to get rolling, but regular practice is what will keep you moving forward. A common belief is that it takes between eight and twelve weeks for a new behavior to become routine. So, just take it easy, don't rush anything and show yourself grace and patience as you try to unlearn whatever the habit is that you are trying to change.

Start a journal

Keeping a journal can help you in many ways, including getting your thoughts organized, facilitating decision making, and, yes, boosting your confidence! In order to boost your self-assurance, consider the following journaling prompts:

Describe ten of your best qualities

Give yourself some praise. Can someone count on you to be a good friend? Do your homemade chocolate chip pancakes rank among the best in the world? Or are you an amazing track star? Put it down on paper! Don't be shy to acknowledge your talents, skills and abilities without hesitation. Go ahead, shine the spotlight on yourself!

Make a daily affirmation list

Yes, give yourself even more praise. Taking the time to praise your own abilities may feel strange at first, but it will pay majorly down the road as your self-belief increases. You have tremendous strength. It takes courage to do what you're doing. Many positive qualities exist within you - these are all the kinds of things you can say to affirm yourself.

List the top ten things you've achieved in your life

You should congratulate yourself! Did your hard work pay off with an A grade? How about the time you took first place in the city's annual writing contest? And that difficult mile run you completed? Every accomplishment is important, so you should take the time to acknowledge and celebrate them. Those who lack confidence in themselves have a tendency to see only the negative aspects of their lives and completely disregard the positive ones. Remember to give yourself credit where credit is due, no matter how big or small the accomplishment!

Write down ten things you're thankful for

The practice of gratitude is a cornerstone of self-assurance. Focusing on what you have to be grateful for can help you stop thinking critically about yourself and others. The grass may not be greener on the side of the street, keep that in mind.

Everyone has something for which to be thankful. We need to remind ourselves of the many blessings in our lives, whether they be good health, a loving family and supportive friends, a comfortable place to sleep, or even just a new day's supply of oxygen. It has been scientifically proven that practicing gratitude raises levels of contentment, motivation, and, once more, general self-esteem. So what are you grateful for today?

Is there anything I can do if I have low self-esteem?

In addition to journaling as mentioned above, there are additional steps you can take to boost your confidence. Never say never; you can always start over. Boosting your confidence can be done by following these suggestions.

Hang out with those who treat you right

Some people constantly bring you down with their actions and words. Friends should be those who make you feel good about who you are, and make you feel encouraged when they say kind things and do nice things for you. Look for friends who will accept you for who you really are, and act as a friend like that to those around you as well.

Tell yourself encouraging things

Get in touch with the thoughts and feelings that are already in you. Is it possible that you're being excessively critical of yourself? Try keeping a journal of your self-talk for a few days. Revisit your list and see what needs to be changed. Are you speaking harshly to yourself? Do these sound like something you'd say to a trusted friend? If you don't like what you see on your list, reword in a way that the things you say are honest, reasonable, and charitable. Review your list frequently. Proceed until adopting a more self-forgiving frame of mind becomes second nature.

Learn to be okay with imperfection

It's a good idea to always try your best, but there is no such thing as being flawless. Perfection is impossible, so learn to be okay with that. Feel proud of yourself for having done your best, and if you find yourself struggling to let go of the demand for perfection, don't hesitate to reach out to a trusted adult for assistance.

Prepare a plan of action and work to achieve it

Do things that are good for you, and you will feel better about yourself. Perhaps you have goals of improving your your academic performance or learning a new instrument. Set a target. The next step after that is to plot out your execution. Do what you set out to do, and keep tabs on how far along you are. Check in on your progress, and celebrate how far you have gotten. Simply tell yourself, "I've been consistent about playing guitar 3 times a week. I'm happy with the results. That pace is sustainable for me."

Pay attention to the positives

Have you been so used to focusing on negatives that they overtake your thoughts? It's easy to dwell on the negative. Negative emotions persist unless they are countered by positive ones. When you find yourself complaining about your day or your life, stop and think before you speak. Think of something positive instead and you might find it brightens your outlook and your mood.

Lend a helping hand

A great and effective way of enhancing your sense of self-worth is by engaging in acts of generosity. Help out a fellow student with their homework, volunteer to pick up litter in your community, or participate in a charity walk. Offer your assistance in the classroom or at home. Be compassionate and try to help others where and when you can. Get involved in activities that highlight the kind of person you are and make you happy with yourself. Your confidence will increase when you take action that improves the world in some way.

Tips for parents

Your teenagers are at a particularly sensitive age, and they face many new and different kinds of pressures. They are experiencing the hormonal transitions of puberty in addition to the social adjustments and upheavals. These factors may contribute significantly to their confusion and struggling sense of self and worth.

However, you shouldn't fret. There are things you can do as a parent to boost your teen's self-esteem and attitude regarding their changing life and circumstances. Here are ten ways to foster a positive outlook and strengthen their foundation.

Cut out the platitudes

Teens have a remarkable ability to see through empty words. They are smart enough to see through your attempts to appease them. Rather than lavishing them with empty platitudes, focus on what they do well and tell them that in all honesty.

Even though their body image is probably of great concern to them at this time, consider coming up with positive affirmations that have nothing to do with your teen's appearance. If you publicly acknowledge their selflessness, generosity, or hard work, you will boost their confidence and feelings of self-worth. Remind them that there are many things about them that have earned your admiration, and that these things are not superficial.

Show your respect and admiration

Is your teen a talented young artist? The act of displaying their latest creation on the fridge will give them a sense of accomplishment and pride no matter their age. Whether they are showing you their latest guitar riff or explaining their current gaming strategy, showing genuine interest and admiration in the things they take pride in and their talents and abilities will help boost their confidence and strengthen your bond.

Teens need to see that you genuinely respect and admire them, not just hear it. Show them, don't just tell them, that you are proud of them and the person they are growing into.

Pay attention to your teenager

Teenagers are social creatures, even when they appear distant. By setting aside quality one-on-one time, you can boost their confidence and sense of worth. They may fight you on this, but stick with it, because that bonding time is crucial in shaping their worldview.

Be reasonable

Your teen probably feels stressed out by the many demands placed upon them, including schoolwork, extracurricular activities, and sports. While self-control is important, there are moments when it's easy to get carried away and overwhelmed by unrelenting discipline.

Let them know you are not looking for perfection from them and instead, instruct them in the art of responsible and practical goal-setting, and demonstrate how to take baby steps toward achieving those goals. They have a lot on their plate already, so let them know they have your support and admiration no matter what challenges they face. Also, if they come to you and let you know they are struggling with too many responsibilities, help them reevaluate their schedule and see if some things can be taken off their plate.

Foster an attitude of self-love and constant development

When you accept yourself, it doesn't mean you're done growing. Even as you reassure your teen that they are wonderful the way they are, you shouldn't dismiss their desire to grow in some areas. Instil in them a healthy sense of self-worth by gently showing them where they excel and where they can continue to seek growth (without being critical). Let them know that growth is a lifelong process, and we are always able to learn and grow, no matter how old we are.

Encourage your teen and applaud their efforts whenever they take a good, healthy risk. Demonstrate to them that self-acceptance and progress are compatible goals.

Discover their passions

Is your teen into basketball? Is there a place in their life and interests for the cheerleading squad, the math club, or the drama club? You don't need to be an expert in their passions to show them your support.

This includes attending games, assisting with practice, and looking for tools that will improve their chances of winning. If you take an interest in their development, you'll improve their confidence and sense of worth, but be sure not to apply too much pressure!

Make it easier for them to help others

One of the best ways to improve one's own sense of worth is to help others. Even for teenagers, this is true. Some teenagers' self-consciousness stems from an unhealthy preoccupation with superficial comparisons to their classmates. It's easy to get caught up in the competition to see who has the newest and greatest gadgets and clothes.

Your teen will gain more than simply the satisfaction of helping others when they venture outside of their comfort zone to do good deeds. As a result, they will view the blessings they have received with new eyes and be grateful for them in ways they hadn't been before, and will have contributed positively to their community.

Teach them to stand up for themselves

Demonstrate to your teen the value of assertiveness and teach them how to use it. The need to learn to stand firm against peer pressure and its effects is something they'll need to master throughout their teen years, and it will serve them well as they learn to set boundaries for themselves now and in the future.

If they develop this skill, your teen will be better able to protect themselves from harm and speak out for themselves and others if they ever experience or witness bullying or mistreatment.

Rephrase negative thoughts

Teens often speak negatively about themselves since they are only echoing their own negative thoughts. In order to help break the loop, you shouldn't immediately demand that they stop.

Instead, try reframing their comments as supportive affirmations. Change negative thoughts like "There's no way I'm going to pass this test" to positive ones like "You can make a decent grade if you study hard."

Lead by example

Children of all ages tend to act like their parents did when they were the same age. They pick up on it when you belittle yourself and your abilities while looking in the mirror, which are probably longstanding habits. Take advantage of your teen's natural tendency to imitate your behavior and set a good example by projecting the kind of self-confidence you would like to see in your teen.

If you want to break the cycle, try looking at each new chance with optimism. Do not be afraid to let your child listen in on you as you discuss your good and bad qualities. They'll pick up the same skills eventually.

Even if it's tempting, refrain from discussing your teen's friends behind their backs. While it's OK to ket your kids vent to you, promoting negative thinking is counterproductive, because it provides the message that it's okay to talk trash about other people. When the conversation heads in that direction, try steering it away from backbiting and focus more on how the situation is making your child feel.

Conclusion

Puberty can bring unexpected changes not only to your body, but also to your emotions, mental health and overall mindset. Puberty is an inescapable rite of passage into adulthood and all the physical, emotional and mental changes you experience during this time are a natural part of this process.

Bodily changes such as growth of breasts, hair and hips, as well as changes like having vaginal discharges and periods are all a part of the natural steps that your body is going through in order to mature into adulthood. Your body will not only grow in these aspects, your height and even your hormones will change and run rampant, sometimes causing mood swings and emotional highs and lows. But there's no need to worry about these things too much since they are all indications that you are maturing, both physically and mentally.

This stage of life can seem tremendously confusing and overwhelming, because of all the ups and downs you're going through. Not only is your body changing, but so are your emotions, your thought processes, and your social world can often be turned upside down as well. It's a lot to go through!

But this book was created to help guide you along the way to make this whole experience easier. You can read it before the changes have started in order to know what to expect, or you can read it while you are in the midst of all of it! Whether you are still waiting to get your first period and are curious about what awaits you, or you've already gotten it and are not quite sure what your body is doing, this book is full of information to help you.

Maybe your friendships are becoming confusing and your relationship with your parents or siblings is becoming more challenging; or perhaps you're struggling with your self-esteem and are searching for new and unique ways to express yourself. Well, these are all completely normal parts of the topsy turvy stage of life known as adolescence. And yup, this book covers all that, too!

So come back to it any time, to get answers or just to feel more understood. Don't worry, you'll make it through all of this, and this book will be right here with you every step of the way!

References

1. Torborg, L. (2018, May 1). *Mayo Clinic Q and A: Gynecologic exams not necessary for all adolescent girls - Mayo Clinic News Network*. Mayo Clinic News Network. Retrieved October 19, 2022, from https://newsnetwork.mayoclinic.org/discussion/mayo-clinic-q-and-a-gynecologic-exams-not-necessary-for-all-adolescent-girls/

2. Vinekar, K. S., Vahratian, A., Hall, K. S., West, B. T., Caldwell, A., Bell, J. D., & Dalton, V. K. (2015, May 27). *Cervical cancer screening, pelvic examinations, and contraceptive use among adolescent and young adult females - PMC*. PubMed Central (PMC). Retrieved October 19, 2022, from https://www.ncbi.nlm.nih.gov/pmc/articles/PMC4580912/

3. Duraccio, K. M., Krietsch, K. N., Chardon, M. L., Van Dyk, T. R., & Beebe, D. W. (2019, September 9). *Poor sleep and adolescent obesity risk: a narrative review of potential mechanisms - PMC*. PubMed Central (PMC). Retrieved October 19, 2022, from https://www.ncbi.nlm.nih.gov/pmc/articles/PMC6749827/

4. Cunningham, R. M., Walton, M. A., & Carter, P. M. (2019, July 18). *The Major Causes of Death in Children and Adolescents in the United States - PMC*. PubMed Central (PMC). Retrieved October 19, 2022, from https://www.ncbi.nlm.nih.gov/pmc/articles/PMC6637963/

5. Ozbay, F., Johnson, D. C., Dimoulas, E., Morgan, I. C., Charney, D., & Southwick, S. (2007, May 1). *Social Support and Resilience to Stress: From Neurobiology to Clinical Practice*. PubMed Central (PMC). Retrieved October 19, 2022, from https://